THE PHEASANT COOK

THE PHEASANT COOK

97 Ways to Present a Bird

TINA DENNIS
AND ROSAMOND CARDIGAN

Line illustrations by Rodger McPhail

The Crowood Press

First published in 1988 by
The Crowood Press
Ramsbury, Marlborough
Wiltshire SN8 2HE

British Library Cataloguing in Publication Data

Dennis, Tina
    The pheasant cook.
    1. Food. Pheasant dishes. Recipes
    I. Title II. Cardigan, Rosamund
    641.6'6596

    ISBN 1–85223–198–X

To our long-suffering husbands . . .

Typeset by Qualitext Typesetting, Abingdon, Oxon
Printed in Great Britain by Billing & Sons Ltd, Worcester

Contents

'Fertile of wood, ashore and Sydney's Copps,
To crown thy open table, doth provide
The Purple Pheasant with the speckled side.'

Ben Jonson, *The Forest*

Introduction

Despite Rodger McPhail's funny cover illustration, *The Pheasant Cook* is a serious cookery book written for everyone who ever needs to cook a pheasant, be they a first-timer or the 'Oh no, not another pheasant' type. We fall into the latter category, both suffering from a severe dose of *Nimius phasianus* during the season; perhaps a luxury for some, but a distinct disadvantage if visits to the butcher make you feel guilty and extravagant! It is often frustrating to go through cookery books trying to find a suitable recipe for the pheasant – they aren't abundant in most books. We thought it might be easier if you only had to refer to one volume – hence the following pages.

We don't pretend to be culinary wizards; this is simply a collection of our favourite recipes – some original, many not – gathered over the years and donated by friends, and adapted and re-adapted. None of them are particularly difficult or time-consuming since we are aiming at the cook in a hurry. Some are extravagant, while others are *bonne femme* and reasonably economical; all are extremely delicious. We have included that old standby, Faisan à la Normande, but our recipe is a more simplified version of the original classic. First courses, pâtés and soups make up only a small section of the book because the pheasant is a main course bird.

As this book is purely about the pheasant, we have been particularly reluctant with our pâtés and terrines. The dryness of the meat needs to be combined with other more succulent game to do justice to these dishes.

We hope that this book will prove useful, and, most importantly, that the recipes will be fun for you to cook.

PS Despite this effort, both our husbands insist that a traditional roast pheasant with all the trimmings is the best eating of all!

CHAPTER 1

THE PHEASANT
(Phasianus Colchicus Linnaeus)

'The pheasant is an enigma, the answer to which is revealed
only to the initiate; they alone can savour it in all its excellence.'
The Philosopher in the Kitchen by
Jean Anthelme Brillat-Savarin

This fine bird, so loved by sportsmen and gourmets alike, is said to have
been discovered by the Argonauts on the banks of the river Phasis in
Colchis, a province of Asia. Hence its name, and such an auspicious
beginning is only suitable for a bird so important in the annals of
sporting history.

The pheasant was introduced to Britain some 800 years ago and
Echards's *History of England* says that in 1299, in the reign of Edward I,
the price of a single bird was 4 pence, whilst a mallard was 3 half-pence
and a plover 1 penny. Even in those far-off days, it was a bird of luxury.
One hundred and twenty years earlier Thomas à Becket, on the day of
his martyrdom, ate it as his last meal. One of his monks recorded that 'he
dined more heartily and cheerfully that day than usual'.

In those days, the pheasant was a totally wild bird but you still needed
a licence to kill it. Today, with shooting such a popular and expensive
sport, the woodland and hedgerows of Great Britain and Northern
Europe abound with stock, more often than not specially reared, fed,
watered and monitored by a keeper. The pheasant is big business and
the old saying 'up goes fifteen shillings, bang goes sixpence and down
comes half a crown' still rings true.

Supermarkets are beginning to stock pheasant and it is starting to
reach a wider market. It may seem a little more expensive than chicken
but it is a good buy, especially as chicken seems so tasteless these days.
Pheasants are genuinely 'free range'!

If you are presented with a brace of pheasants they must be hung for at
least 5–10 days, to allow their special gamey flavour to develop, before
they can be plucked and drawn. They should be hung by their heads in a
cool, dry place, preferably in fresh air, until the breast feathers can be
easily pulled out and they smell 'done'. When you are given pheasants,
you are at the mercy of the donor as to whether they are young or old. If

you can choose your own, however, pick a young one — it is always the most tender — and remember too that a hen makes better eating (despite being smaller), having flesh that is less tough and more succulent. To tell the age of a cock pheasant early in the season, look at the spurs — the longer and sharper they are, the older the bird. Unfortunately, this can only be applied at the beginning of the season, as the spurs of young and old birds become increasingly alike towards the end. The only really accurate way of telling the age of a pheasant is to apply the rather complicated bursa test, which is described in *The Complete Book of Game Conservation*, published by Stanley Paul.

PLUCKING AND DRAWING

Always pluck against the lie of the feathers, from tail to head. Hold the feathers tightly between your thumb and bent index finger. Work quickly and carefully, taking care not to tear the skin, especially around the shot areas. Sometimes tweezers are helpful on the smaller, more stubborn feathers. (Many of the recipes in this book call for pheasant without skin, so you can, on occasions, skin the pheasant completely, feathers and all. This is a much quicker and cleaner operation all round.) After plucking, the remaining feathers and down should be singed off with a lighted candle, taking care not to blacken the skin.

To draw the bird, lay it on its back and cut off the head, leaving about 5cm (2in) of neck. Cut the skin on the underside of the neck, loosen it and pull it back. Cut off the remaining piece of neck close to the body. Remove the crop carefully so as not to break it and cut out the windpipe and any deposits of fat. Insert your hand, palm down, into the body cavity and loosen the entrails. Make a small slit in the other end of the bird (the vent end) and, with the other hand, pull out all the innards. Discard the bitter gall bladder and retain the rest of the entrails for stock. Rinse inside and out and wipe the pheasant thoroughly. The smaller the holes you make in the bird the better prepared it is, so people with little hands tend to make the best drawers. However, this shouldn't be used as an excuse by those with large hands to shirk this least popular of tasks!

Pheasant, and indeed all game birds, are served with their feet left on, and certainly a pheasant that is neatly trussed, with its ankles crossed and feet intact, has a special smartness. However, many would dis-

agree and it is not so common now to see them served in this traditional way. To remove your pheasant's feet, twist and break the bone at the base of each drum stick, work loose and pull away the tendons. Then cut through the skin and bone just above the foot and discard.

TRUSSING

Trussing is done to keep the bird's shape during cooking so that it can be tidily brought to the table. However, trussing a pheasant is not quite as simple as trussing a chicken. Usually, unless you are lucky enough to have a bird shot through the head, the body has been damaged in the killing – legs may be shattered, wings missing or skin torn. In such cases, an intelligent bit of DIY with skewers and cocktail sticks is the best and quickest method, helped along with a bit of *Gros point* with a trussing needle and string. If you are a stickler for detail, or have a perfectly shot and cleaned bird, the best way to learn how to truss is to follow diagrams (excellent in *Reader's Digest* cookery books) or to be shown by a master. If you are roasting your pheasant for an informal do, or planning to carve it before you bring it to the table, don't bother to truss it – it really doesn't matter in that case if its legs are sticking out at right angles.

CHAPTER 2

STOCK AND SOUPS

Many of the recipes in this book call for a pheasant stock and it really is worth the effort to make your own. A well-made stock does give a dish that little something extra.

Stock can be made from raw or cooked bones and the recipes on the following pages will always leave you with a carcass for your base. You might find the stock made from cooked bones not quite strong enough – if so, add a chicken stock cube, a piece of bacon, some left-over gravy or a glass of wine. Don't ever throw a carcass away – freeze it for later if you haven't time to make the stock immediately (Note *Don't do this if it's raw and has been already frozen.*) In the same way, freeze any left-over stock you may have in ice trays or yoghurt cartons – there are so many dishes that call for small quantities. A stock will last for about four days in the refrigerator but should be boiled up daily if it contains any green vegetables, otherwise it may turn sour.

We too often reach for the stock cube these days – wonderful when you're in a hurry but no substitute for the real thing.

The best stocks are made from all the odd bits and pieces that litter the fridge in little pots and on saucers – too good to throw away and too small to make a meal on their own. Traditionally, these were added to the stock-pot that continually bubbled on the stove, and in this way a marvellous, rich and delicious soup was always at hand, ready to enhance a stew or just be a quick and nourishing meal in itself.

There follows a very basic, traditional recipe for pheasant stock that we hope you will doctor and adapt as your own.

Pheasant Stock

2 carrots, roughly chopped
2 onions, roughly chopped
2 stalks celery, roughly chopped
4 large sprigs parsley
2 bay leaves
1 sprig thyme
8 peppercorns
½ teaspoon salt

1 Put all the ingredients in a large saucepan and cover with cold water. Bring to the boil and skim off any scum that appears on the surface. Cover and simmer for 3 hours.

2 Reduce, strain and keep in a cold place.

3 The next day remove any surface fat.

As pheasant stock has a distinct gamey flavour, it is delicious in many soups but, equally, disastrous in others. It tends to lend itself better to the 'winter warmers' rather than the light summer soups. Some of the recipes which follow are classic soups, which we have found successful with a game stock.

Consommé

Serves 8–10

This recipe is included because it is extremely easy to make and not at all time-consuming.

Serve hot, laced with sherry. It may be necessary to add two leaves of gelatine, depending on the quality of your stock, for a cold jellied soup.

1.1 litres/2 pints cold pheasant
  stock

Clearing ingredients:
450g/1lb best mince
2 leeks, finely chopped
2 carrots, finely chopped
2 celery sticks, finely chopped
handful parsley
6 egg whites, whisked in a little
  water
salt and black pepper

---

1 Using a large pan, put all the ingredients into the cold stock and season well. Stir whilst the mixture warms up. Once it becomes cloudy, stop stirring.

---

2 Boil the mixture for at least 10 minutes until the egg has set on the surface. You will be able to tell when the liquor has cleared by gently testing with a spoon.

---

3 Strain the liquid through a clean tea cloth into a bowl. Discard the meat and vegetables, which by this time are quite tasteless.

Consommé à la Paysanne

Serves 6

This is very pretty, adding an extra dimension to clear soup.

1.1 litres/2 pints consommé (see
  page 15)
100g/4oz carrots, peeled
100g/4oz french beans
100g/4oz petit pois
40g/1½oz butter
½ glass sherry

1 Square the carrots and slice very thin. Cut the beans into 1cm (½in) lengths. Cook the vegetables separately in boiling salted water until just tender. Drain and refresh under a cold tap. Shake vegetables in melted butter.

2 Reheat the consommé, add the sherry and the vegetables. Keep hot in a tureen. Alternatively, put the vegetables into bowls and pour the consommé over.

Pheasant Consommé Madrilène

Serves 4

An unusual and refreshing start to a meal – this should be served cold with a small glass of Russian vodka as a special dinner party starter.

1.1 litres/2 pints stock made from
*   pheasant carcass*
clearing ingredients as for
*   consommé recipe*
1 teaspoon tomato purée
6 tomatoes, skinned, pipped and
*   chopped*
½ glass sherry
2 leaves gelatine, softened in cold
*   water*
salt and pepper

---

1 Clear the stock as described for Consommé (*see* page 15), but add the gelatine, the skins and pips of the tomatoes and the purée. Allow gelatine to melt and then pass through a cloth into a bowl.

---

2 Reheat the consommé. Add the sherry and remove from heat. Add the tomatoes and allow the consommé to cool.

Stilton Cheese Soup

Serves 4–6

An excellent way of using up all those leftover bits of Stilton.

1 onion, chopped finely
75g/3oz butter
175g/6oz Stilton cheese, crumbled
75g/3oz flour
1.1 litres/2 pints pheasant stock
1 bay leaf
150ml/¼ pint single cream
salt and black pepper

1 In a saucepan, melt the butter and fry the onion until soft. Stir in the Stilton until it melts, then add the flour. Cook for 5 minutes, stirring constantly.

2 Add the stock, bay leaf and seasoning. Bring to the boil, stir well, cover and simmer for 20 minutes. Remove the bay leaf, blend in the cream, check seasoning and serve immediately.

Mulligatawny Soup

Serves 4–6

A warming soup – especially when drunk from a Thermos after a mid-morning drive in an open field blasted by an easterly wind!

1 large onion, chopped
1 carrot, chopped
2 stalks celery, chopped
1 cooking apple, peeled, cored
*   and chopped*
50g/2oz butter
1 tablespoon curry paste
25g/1oz flour
1 tablespoon tomato purée
1.1 litres/2 pints pheasant stock
2 sprigs parsley
1 tablespoon shredded coconut
1 teaspoon brown sugar
3 teaspoons lemon juice
4 tablespoons cooked rice
salt and pepper

---

1 In a saucepan, melt the butter and sauté the onion, carrot, celery and cooking apple until soft and golden. Add the curry paste, then the flour and cook, stirring all the time, for 5 minutes. Add the tomato pureé, then the stock, herbs, seasoning, coconut and sugar. Stir well, cover and simmer for 45 minutes.

---

2 Liquidise, then return to the heat and add the rice and lemon juice. Reheat thoroughly.

Green Lentil Soup

Serves 4–6

1 large onion, chopped
2 carrots, chopped
2 stalks celery, chopped
2 rashers back bacon, rind
*   removed*
25g/1oz butter
225g/8oz green lentils
*   (thoroughly washed and*
*   soaked overnight)*
3 sprigs parsley
1.1 litres/2 pints pheasant stock
salt and pepper

1 In a saucepan, melt the butter and sauté the onion, carrots, celery and bacon. Add the stock, lentils, parsley and seasoning. Stir well and simmer, covered, for 2 hours, or until the lentils are cooked.

2 Liquidise, check seasoning and serve very hot with a garnish of fried bread croûtons.

Cream of Chestnut Soup

Serves 4–6

For the soup:
50g/2oz butter
1 large onion, sliced
1 large carrot, peeled and sliced
1 stalk celery, sliced
1 large can chestnut purée
1.1 litres/2 pints pheasant stock
1 tablespoon parsley, chopped
pinch thyme
pinch nutmeg
275ml/½ pint single cream
salt and pepper

For the garnish:
2 cooking apples, peeled, cored
   and sliced.

1 Melt the butter in a saucepan and sauté the onion, carrot and celery for a few minutes without browning. Stir in the chestnut purée and blend well. Add the stock, herbs, nutmeg and seasoning, stir well and simmer for 30 minutes or until the vegetables are tender.

2 Liquidise the soup, return to the heat and stir in the cream.

3 For the garnish, fry the slices of apple in butter and sprinkle them with demerara sugar. Check the seasoning of the soup and serve hot in individual bowls garnished with one or two slices of fried apple.

Celery Soup

Serves 4–6

For the soup:
1 slice bacon, chopped
50g/2oz butter
350g/12oz celery, sliced finely
1 large onion, chopped
1 potato, peeled and diced
1 tablespoon flour
1.1 litres/2 pints pheasant stock
1 bay leaf
3 sprigs parsley
pinch thyme
salt and pepper
2 tablespoons crème fraîche

For the garnish:
2 tablespoons chopped fried
    bacon
crème fraîche
cayenne pepper

1 Melt the butter in a saucepan and sauté the bacon, celery, onion and potato
   for a few minutes, stirring constantly to prevent browning. Add the flour and
   cook for a further 2 minutes. Add the stock and herbs and simmer for about
   30 minutes or until the vegetables are tender. Check seasoning and blend in
   the crème fraîche.

2 Serve in individual bowls and decorate with blobs of crème fraîche, bacon,
   croûtons and cayenne pepper.

Jerusalem Artichoke Cream

Serves 4–6

450g/1lb Jerusalem artichokes,
*   peeled and sliced*
1 onion, sliced
1 stalk celery, sliced
50g/2oz butter
25g/1oz flour
1 bouquet garni
1.1 litres/2 pints pheasant stock
150ml/¼ pint double cream
salt and black pepper

1 In a saucepan, melt the butter and sauté the artichokes, onion and celery for 5 minutes, stirring constantly to prevent browning. Add the flour and cook for a further 2 minutes. Add the stock and bouquet garni and simmer for 30 minutes, or until the vegetables are tender.

2 Remove the bouquet garni and liquidise the soup. Return to the heat and stir in the cream. Season.

Cock-a-Leekie Soup

Serves 6–8

A variation on an old theme and a meal in itself.

For the stock:
1 pheasant
1 onion
2 carrots
1 stalk celery
6 peppercorns
1 bouquet garni
3 sprigs parsley
2 bay leaves

For the soup:
6 leeks (white part only), sliced
450g/1lb prunes, stoned and
*   soaked overnight*
salt and black pepper
2 carrots, sliced
1 heaped tablespoon rice
1 tablespoon chopped parsley

---

1 Put all the stock ingredients into a large saucepan and cover with cold water. Add salt and bring to the boil. Cover and simmer for 2 hours, removing any scum that comes to the surface. Remove the pheasant, strain the stock and set aside.

---

2 Put the leeks, prunes and sliced carrots in a pan and add 1.5 litres (2½ pints) of the pheasant stock. Cook for 10 minutes. Add the rice, stir well and cook for a further 20 minutes.

---

3 Meanwhile, remove the meat from the pheasant and chop. Add as much as you want to the soup along with the chopped parsley. Reheat, check seasoning and serve with brown bread and butter.

Beetroot Soup

Serves 4–6

This soup is such a rich and beautiful colour. It is lovely served in simple traditional china soup plates on a table covered with a white damask cloth.

450g/1lb raw beetroots, peeled
  and chopped (wear rubber
  gloves to do this)
1 large onion, chopped
1.1 litres/2 pints pheasant stock
2 tablespoons lemon juice
1 glass sherry
salt and black pepper
sour cream to garnish

1 Put the onion and beetroot in a saucepan with the stock, bring to the boil and simmer, covered, for 45 minutes, or until the beetroot is cooked.

2 Liquidise and return to the heat. Add lemon juice, sherry and seasoning and reheat thoroughly.

3 Serve in individual bowls garnished with a trail of sour cream floating on top.

Cream of Pheasant Soup

Serves 4–6

1 onion, chopped
2 stalks celery, finely sliced
5 button mushrooms, wiped and
*   sliced*
50g/2oz butter
25g/1oz flour
1.1 litres/2 pints pheasant stock
1 bouquet garni
pinch of mace
100g/4oz cooked pheasant, finely
*   chopped*
2 egg yolks
150ml/¼ pint cream
salt and pepper
1 tablespoon parsley, chopped for
*   garnish*

1 Melt the butter in a saucepan and gently sauté the onion, celery and mushrooms. Sprinkle with flour and stir well. Add the stock, herbs and seasoning, blend well, then simmer with a lid on for 30 minutes, stirring occasionally.

2 Remove the bouquet garni and liquidise. Return the soup to the heat and add the pheasant meat.

3 Mix together the egg yolks and cream to make the liaison and add to this a few spoonfuls of hot soup (this will prevent curdling). Mix well and strain back into the soup, stirring all the time. Do not allow the soup to boil or it will curdle.

4 Serve garnished with the chopped parsley.

Spicy Pheasant Soup

Serves 4–6

40g/1½oz butter
1 red pepper, seeded and
    chopped
1 onion, chopped
25g/1oz flour
1 tablespoon tomato purée
425g/15oz can chopped tomatoes
1 bouquet garni
1.1 litres/2 pints pheasant stock
½ teaspoon cayenne pepper
½ teaspoon paprika
¼ teaspoon sugar
1 teaspoon vinegar
2 teaspoons grated horseradish
175g/6oz cooked pheasant,
    minced
salt and pepper

---

1 Melt the butter in a soup pot and sauté the pepper and onion until soft. Add the flour and cook for 1 minute.

---

2 Stir in the tomato purée, tomatoes and bouquet garni, stock and seasoning. Simmer for 30 minutes.

---

3 Remove the bouquet garni and add the cayenne pepper, paprika, sugar, vinegar, grated horseradish and pheasant meat. Stir and cook for a further 3 minutes or until the meat is heated through. Serve very hot with crusty bread.

Pheasant Gumbo

Serves 4–6

An extremely unusual soup. Serve it as a light lunch and show everyone how original you are!

2 shallots, chopped
40g/1¹/₂oz butter
400g/14oz can of chopped
*   tomatoes*
¹/₂ green pepper, seeded and
*   chopped*
400g/14oz can okra, drained
2 tablespoons rice
1.1 litres/2 pints pheasant stock
225g/8oz cooked pheasant meat,
*   finely chopped*
75g/3oz tinned sweetcorn
2 tablespoons parsley, chopped

1 Sauté the shallots with the butter in a saucepan. Add the tomatoes, pepper, okra, rice and stock. Season and stir well. Cover and simmer very gently for 30 minutes.

2 Add the pheasant meat and the sweetcorn and cook for a further 3 minutes to heat the meat through. Serve garnished with the chopped parsley.

Traditional Pheasant Soup

Serves 4–6

50g/2oz butter
1 onion, finely chopped
2 carrots, finely chopped
2 stalks celery, very finely sliced
2 tablespoons flour
1.1 litres/2 pints good pheasant
*   stock*
1 bouquet garni
1 tablespoon redcurrant jelly
1 glass port
175g/6oz cooked pheasant meat,
*   very finely shredded*
1 tablespoon parsley, finely
*   chopped*
salt and pepper

1 Melt the butter and fry the onion, carrots and celery until just golden. Stir in
   the flour and cook for 1 minute more. Pour in the stock and stir to blend. Add
   the bouquet garni and seasoning and simmer for 15 minutes.

2 Add the redcurrant jelly, port and pheasant meat and cook for a further 5
   minutes.

3 Remove the bouquet garni and sprinkle with parsley before serving.

Cream of Curried Pheasant and Lentil Soup

Served 4–6

225g/8oz cooked pheasant meat,
   finely chopped
1.1 litres/2 pints pheasant stock
100g/4oz lentils, soaked overnight
1 onion, chopped
1 leek, sliced
25g/1oz butter
1 eating apple, peeled, cored and
   chopped
1 tablespoon mango chutney
¼ teaspoon powdered mace
1 dessertspoon curry powder
100ml/3½fl oz double cream
salt and pepper

1 Sauté the onion and leek in the butter and add the curry powder and mace.

2 Stir in the stock, lentils, apple, chutney and seasoning, simmer for 1 hour.

3 Add the pheasant and cream and cook for 1 minute.

4 Liquidise and serve piping hot with spicy poppadoms.

Sauerkraut Soup

Serves 4–6

1 onion, chopped
1 large carrot, sliced
1 potato, peeled and sliced
50g/2oz butter
25g/1oz flour
1 teaspoon tomato purée
350g/12oz prepared (tinned)
    sauerkraut
1 tablespoon parsley, chopped
1 teaspoon chervil, chopped
1 litre/1¾ pints pheasant stock
salt and pepper
sour cream

1 Melt the butter in a saucepan and sauté the onion, carrot and potato until golden. Stir in the flour and cook for 2 minutes.

2 Add the tomato purée, sauerkraut and herbs. Cook for a further 2 minutes then add the stock. Simmer for 35 minutes, or until the carrots and potatoes are soft. Season to taste and serve in hot bowls with a blob of sour cream on top.

Curried Parsnip Soup

Serves 4–6

A light and delicate soup – a great favourite!

450g/1lb parsnips, peeled and
  finely sliced
1 onion, chopped
50g/2oz butter
1 tablespoon mild curry paste
15g/¹/₂oz flour
1 litre/1³/₄ pints pheasant stock
1 tablespoon parsley, chopped
pinch of thyme
2 tablespoons crème fraîche
salt

1 Melt the butter in a saucepan and sauté the parsnips and onion until soft – about 5 minutes. Stir in the curry paste, then the flour, and blend well. Add stock, herbs and salt to taste.

2 Simmer for 30 minutes, stirring occasionally. Blend until smooth in a liquidiser. Add the crème fraîche and blend again.

3 Return to the heat for a few minutes and check seasoning. Serve with poppadoms or chapatis instead of bread.

CHAPTER 3

STARTERS AND
MAIN COURSES

'Fesaunt exceedeth all foules in sweetness and
wholesomenesse and is equal to a capon in nourishing
. . . it is meate for princes and great estates and for
poore schollers when they can get it.'
                    Cogan's *Haven of Health*, London 1612

As we said in the introduction, pheasant is traditionally a main course
dish, and you will therefore find very few ideas for first courses on the
following pages. Some of the salads could possibly be served as starters,
using smaller quantities, but people usually find that the rather
dominant flavour of pheasant means that it is better suited as the
principal part of the menu than as a prelude to another dish. The dryness
of the flesh also tends to exclude its use in pâtés or terrines, unless it is
combined with other meats, so there are hardly any pure pheasant pâtés
here.

Retaining the moisture is paramount when you are cooking a
pheasant. The great Escoffier suggests that we don't lard the meat – a
young, tender, well-hung bird will not need it, and an old bird will not
be worth the trouble, being fit only for stocks and stews. However, extra
care should be taken with your pheasant when you are cooking it. You
cannot simply load the bird into the oven and forget about it, especially
when you are roasting, when you must remember to baste very often.
Investing in a chicken brick (*see* page 42) is strongly recommended.

A carefully prepared pheasant really is a king of dishes.

Pheasant Pâté en Croûte

Serves 8

Ask your butcher to bone the fattest hen you have – it's much quicker if he does it, and his knives are sharper. Ask him to reserve the liver.

1 fat hen
275g/10oz pork
175g/6oz veal
125ml/4fl oz brandy
75ml/3 fl oz port
1 egg, beaten
25g/1oz butter
450g/1lb short pastry
6 chipolatas, skinned and sliced
100g/4oz bacon, cut into strips
1 egg, beaten

Pre-heat oven to 190°C/375°F/Gas Mark 5.

---

1 Cut the breasts into thick fillets. Mince the remaining meat and mix with the pork and veal. Season well and add the brandy, port and egg. Sauté the liver in butter and add a dash of brandy when cooked.

---

2 Roll out the pastry and line a loaf tin. Trim, leaving at least 1cm (½in) overlap at top edges. Use trimmings for top by pressing together and rolling to fit.

---

3 Place half of the mince in the bottom. Add layers of breasts, roughly chopped liver, chipolatas and bacon. Pour over the juices from the liver marinade. Finish with remaining mince. Press well with fingers.

---

4 Wet pastry edges and cover with remaining pastry. Pinch edges. Decorate top with pastry leaves and brush with beaten egg. Make a funnel with a postcard and stick in the middle to allow the steam to escape.

---

5 Bake for 1¼ hours. Place on wire rack to cool before unmoulding. Serve cold.

Pheasant Egg au Naturel

These may be obtained from someone who rears pheasants for shooting and who may often have many eggs surplus to requirements. They could be eaten before dinner with drinks, and may be served warm.

2–3 eggs per person
celery salt
black pepper

1 Boil the eggs for 3 minutes. Leave in cold water to cool.

2 Arrange in bowls with celery salt and black pepper.

Pheasant Egg Mousse

Serves 6

This mousse is very rich and a beautiful bright yellow in colour. I usually serve it with strips of cold fried bread or a crispbread.

For the mousse:
*225g/8oz pheasant eggs, hard
    boiled*
150ml/¼ pint mayonnaise
50g/2oz jellied consommé
*2 leaves gelatine, softened in cold
    water*
*50ml/2fl oz double cream,
    whipped*
handful chopped parsley

For the garnish:
tiny tomatoes
black olives
parsley and mint leaves

---

1 Chop the eggs roughly and mix with mayonnaise and consommé. Season well.

---

2 Melt the gelatine in a little hot water and add to the mixture. Allow the mixture to start to set.

---

3 Fold in the cream and the parsley and spoon into a soufflé dish. Leave in a cold place until set.

Pheasant Egg Mayonnaise

These can be added to crudités in summer and can be an alternative to bantam or quail eggs. A few could be used as a garnish for other recipes.

8 eggs, boiled, cracked and
  peeled
1–2 tablespoons mayonnaise
celery salt
black pepper
1 tablespoon parsley (optional)
parsley or chervil to garnish

1 Halve the eggs, remove the yolks and mash up with the remaining ingredients. Season well.

2 Spoon the mixture into the halves and scatter over chopped parsley or chervil.

Pheasant and Rabbit Terrine

Serves 8

An adaptation from the game terrine in *Recipes for Success*. This has the virtue of keeping for at least a week in the refrigerator. It does shrink from the sides of the container, but looks very attractive when turned on to the plate.

1 rabbit, meat cut into strips
1 pheasant, meat cut into strips
12 rashers bacon
225g/8oz lambs liver
225g/8oz sausagemeat
1 large onion, chopped
6 tablespoons parsley, chopped
1 egg and 1 tablespoon milk,
*   mixed together*
6 tablespoons breadcrumbs
seasoning
port or brandy
bay leaves

Pre-heat oven to 180°C/350°F/Gas Mark 4.

---

1 Line a terrine with the bacon, reserving some for the top.

---

2 Mash or blend together the livers and sausagemeat. Mix well with the onions, parsley, egg and milk and breadcrumbs. Season well and add the port or brandy.

---

3 Place half the mixture in the terrine. Press strips of rabbit and pheasant into the mixture. Cover with the remaining mixture and press down well. Decorate the top with bay leaves and cover with the remaining bacon. Cover with foil and cook in a bain-marie for 1½ hours at 180°C/350°F/Gas Mark 4.

---

4 When cooked, leave to cool overnight, with weight on top to compress the mixture. Remove the bay leaves before serving. Turn into a bowl or on to a plate and serve with toast or French bread.

Traditional Roast Pheasant with all the Trimmings

Method One – In the Roasting Tin

Serves 4

The following two cooking methods will produce equally delicious results. Choose which one you prefer whenever a recipe calls for roasting the pheasant.

1 pheasant
5 rashers streaky bacon
½ onion
3 sprigs parsley
knob of butter
flour
salt and pepper

For the gravy:
1 glass red wine
275ml/½ pint pheasant stock or
  vegetable water
1 tablespoon redcurrant jelly

Pre-heat the oven to 200°C/400°F/Gas Mark 6.

---

1 Wipe the pheasant inside and out and stuff the cavity with the onion, parsley, butter, seasoning, and 2 rashers of bacon. Truss as for roasting chicken, season and place breast-down in a well-greased roasting tin. Cover with the remaining bacon and roast for 30 minutes.

---

2 Turn the pheasant the right way up. Removing the bacon, baste the breasts and sprinkle with flour. Cook for a further 15–20 minutes until the breasts are brown and pheasant juices are running clear when you insert a skewer in the leg. Remove the pheasant to a serving dish and keep warm.

---

3 To make the gravy, pour away any fat in the tin and scrape up all the cooking juices with the red wine. Add the stock and reduce by one-third. Stir in the redcurrant jelly and heat through. Check seasoning and strain into a sauce-boat.

Traditional Roast Pheasant with all the Trimmings

Method Two – In the Chicken Brick

Serves 4

This method is mentioned in many of the recipes. The pheasant will be succulent and falling off the bone. It will keep in the brick for at least half an hour without any adverse effect.

1 pheasant, well seasoned inside   *wine*
    with a whole onion   *stock*

Pre-heat oven to 200°C/400°F/Gas Mark 6.

---

1 Submerge the brick in water for an hour.

---

2 Place the bird in the brick and bake for 1 hour.

---

3 Remove bird and carve or joint.

---

4 Carefully pour off any grease, pour the juices into a pan and add some wine or stock. Heat through and season. Hand the gravy separately.

Suggested Trimmings

Bread sauce   *Fried breadcrumbs*
Bacon curls   *Chipolatas*
Game chips   *Roasted chestnuts*
Redcurrant jelly   *Cranberry sauce*

Bread sauce and breadcrumbs can be made in bulk and successfully frozen in the required amounts. This is to be recommended as they are the most called for and also the most time-consuming of all the trimmings.

Serving Suggestion for a Dinner Party

Pheasant looks very grand decorated with its own tail feathers – especially those from the cock bird. They should be washed and dried in a very cool oven or the airing cupboard, then inserted fan-wise in the vent end of the cooked bird.

Chinese Pheasant

Serves 8

This dish can be prepared well in advance and reheated. Present it at the table in a casserole or similar dish with chervil scattered over the top. Serve with plain rice, or more extravagantly, wild rice and a green salad.

8 breasts from 2 brace of
  pheasants
dry sherry
2–3 tablespoons soy sauce
3 tablespoons sunflower oil
275g/10oz ginger, fresh and
  grated
5 cloves garlic
100g/4oz tin black beans in sauce
vegetable stock
3 tablespoons chervil, chopped

---

1 Shred the flesh into finger-sized strips. (The wing can also be used if necessary.) Marinate overnight in enough dry sherry to cover and the soy sauce.

---

2 After 24 hours, heat the oil in a large pan and fry the ginger and garlic for a few minutes. Add the strips of meat and sauté for a further 5 minutes. Add the beans and warm them through.

---

3 Add enough stock to cover all the ingredients and simmer for a further 5 minutes, or until cooked.

Pheasant Tarragon

Serves 6

You must use fresh tarragon for this recipe. Pheasant braised on a bed of vegetables benefits from this method, becoming particularly succulent. This dish will keep for at least 45 minutes without spoiling if it is well covered.

brace of pheasant
100g/4oz butter
2–3 teaspoons dried tarragon or
*   20 fresh leaves*
2 carrots, sliced
1 onion, sliced
salt and pepper
stock
wine glass of Madeira

Pre-heat the oven to 200°C/400°F/Gas Mark 6.

---

1 Brown the birds in 50g (2oz) butter in a frying pan. Discard the butter since it inevitably browns and will spoil the flavour of the sauce.

---

2 Melt a further 50g (2oz) butter in a deep casserole and sauté the vegetables for a few minutes. Add the herbs and season well. Place the birds on the top, cover them in foil and bake for 30 minutes (for a young bird).

---

3 When cooked remove the birds, carve and keep them warm.

---

4 Purée the vegetables in a blender or vegetable mill.

---

5 Pour a little stock into the casserole and place it over the heat, stirring well to mix in all the juices from the roasting. Add some of the puréed vegetables and stock until the sauce reaches the desired consistency. Add the Madeira, adjust the seasoning and add extra fresh herbs as desired. Pour the sauce over the meat and garnish with parsley.

Pheasant with Spanish Rice

Makes 6

1 pheasant, jointed
seasoned flour
3 shallots, finely chopped
1 green pepper, sliced
3 cloves garlic
350g/12oz rice with a pinch of
    saffron
pheasant stock to cover
1 tablespoon tomato purée
400g/14oz tin tomatoes
175g/6oz chorizos, sliced
parsley, chopped

Pre-heat the oven to 190°C/375°F/Gas Mark 5.

---

1 Dip the joints in seasoned flour and fry until brown. Remove.

---

2 Fry the shallots and pepper and, lastly, the garlic for a few seconds.

---

3 Return the joints, add the rice, stock to cover, the tomato purée and the tomatoes. Cover with greaseproof paper and a lid and cook for one hour.

---

4 Add the chorizos in the last 20 minutes, when the pheasant is ready and arranged on a dish. Scatter parsley over.

Pheasant Breast with Sorrel and Watercress Sauce

Makes 4

A 'designer' sauce! A beautiful colour and the two vegetables complement each other's flavours well.

4 pheasant breasts
50g/2oz butter
25g/1oz chervil
1 shallot, chopped
450g/1lb sorrel
2 bunches watercress
150ml/¼ pint stock
150ml/¼ pint cream
watercress to garnish

Pre-heat oven to highest setting.

1 Wrap seasoned pheasants in foil with some butter and some chervil and cook for 15 to 20 minutes.

2 Sauté the shallot in butter until transparent, add the sorrel and watercress and stock. Season. When soft liquidise and add cream.

3 When pheasant breasts are ready, add the juices to the sauce and mix well.

4 Pour sauce on to deep meat dish, arrange pheasant breasts on top and garnish with watercress.

Pheasant with Pinot Mushrooms and Chestnuts

Makes 4

You could substitute Madeira or Marsala for the Pinot.

4 pheasant breasts on the bone
25g/1oz butter
25ml/1fl oz oil
12 chestnuts (frozen), peeled
225g/8oz button mushrooms
stock
225ml/8fl oz Pinot
seasoning

1 Brown the pheasant in the butter and oil and then cook very slowly on a low heat.

2 Simmer the chestnuts in some stock. When almost cooked, add the mushrooms.

3 Arrange the pheasants on a dish with the mushrooms and the chestnuts.

4 Pour away excess fat from juices, add the Pinot and reheat. Adjust seasoning and pour over the meat.

Bonfire Pheasant

This is *the* way to cook pheasants. The success of this recipe is due to the intense heat of the fire searing and sealing the meat. Although the outsides are sometimes burnt, the insides are perfect. We cook over the hot embers, no charcoal for us.

pheasant, jointed and barbecued

For the sauce:
3–4 tablespoons honey
3–4 tablespoons redcurrant jelly
3 tablespoons tomato ketchup
1 tablespoon tomato purée
2–3 tablespoons soy sauce
3 tablespoons red wine vinegar
425ml/³⁄₄ pint pheasant stock
port
herbs

1 Mix all the sauce ingredients together and season. Reduce to a thick syrup. Adjust with a dash of port and reheat when required.

2 Keep in a jug near the bonfire. The sauce need not be hot since the meat will be!

3 Either pour over cooked joints or dip the meat into the sauce.

Frenchly Pheasant

Serves 4

An extremely easy and relatively quick casserole, to be served with mashed potato.

1 pheasant, quartered
100g/4oz butter
1 onion, finely chopped
2 carrots, thinly sliced
6 cloves garlic, crushed
1 can game soup
2 oranges, squeezed for their
*   juice*
1 tin crushed tomatoes
1 tablespoon each thyme and
*   basil*
4 courgettes, sliced, salted and
*   blanched*
1 green pepper, cut into strips
*   and blanched*

---

1 Sauté the pieces of pheasant in butter in a heavy casserole for 10 minutes. Remove. Add the vegetables and garlic and cook for a further 10 minutes. Replace the pheasant.

---

2 Pour on the soup, orange juice, tomatoes and herbs. Simmer for 30–40 minutes.

---

3 Meanwhile, in a separate pan cook the courgettes and peppers in butter, and when cooked add to the casserole.

Pheasant with Blackcurrants and Cassis

Makes 8

You could use blackberries instead of blackcurrants – either way, the sauce is a glorious colour. Serve with wild rice and green salad.

2 pheasants, quartered
225ml/8 fl oz fruit vinegar
3 tablespoons fresh thyme,
   chopped
3 tablespoons fresh applemint,
   chopped
450g/1lb jar of blackcurrant jelly
450g/1lb blackcurrants, soaked
   in cassis to cover

Pre-heat oven to 190°C/375°F/Gas Mark 5.

---

1 Marinate the pheasants for half a day in vinegar and herbs.

---

2 Arrange meat in a roasting dish and cover with jelly and fruits. Sprinkle on the marinade. Cover with foil and bake in the oven for 30 minutes.

---

3 Remove the pheasants to a warm dish. Stir in the juices over the heat and season; reduce if necessary and add a dash more cassis to taste. pour over the meat and scatter on the parsley.

Pheasant with Raspberries

Makes 4

An interesting way to deal with pheasant from the freezer.

4 pheasant breasts
100g/4oz butter
2 onions, finely chopped
6 tablespoons raspberry vinegar
1 glass wine
225ml/8fl oz stock or water
275ml/½ pint double cream
275g/10oz tin crushed tomatoes
raspberries to garnish

1 Sauté the breasts in the butter for about 5 minutes. Remove and keep warm.

2 Cook the onion in the same pan until transparent, add the vinegar and reduce until syrupy. Stir in the wine, stock, cream and tomatoes and heat. Season well.

3 Add the pheasant and cook for a further 5–10 minutes until done. Remove pheasant to a warm serving dish and reduce the sauce if necessary. Scatter the raspberries over and serve.

Marinated Pheasant with Prunes, Olives and Capers

Makes 8

2 pheasants, quartered

For the marinade:
175g/6oz brown sugar
2 glasses white wine
handful of parsley and chervil
vinegar
oil
8 cloves garlic, crushed
6 tablespoons oregano, fresh
6 tablespoons thyme, fresh
3 bay leaves
20 prunes, pitted
20 olives, black or green
175g/6oz capers
salt and pepper

Pre-heat oven to 200°C/400°F/Gas Mark 6.

---

1 Marinate the pheasant pieces in the marinade ingredients and leave overnight.

---

2 Arrange pieces in layers in a shallow oven-proof dish, pour on marinade, sprinkle with brown sugar and pour on wine. Bake in the oven for about 30 minutes or until done.

---

3 Serve from the dish, with wild rice, and scatter on the parsley and chervil.

Pheasant with Leek and Nuts

Serves 8

A scrumptious recipe from America.

2 pheasants, preferably hens
100g/4oz butter
8 bacon rashers
2 carrots, thinly sliced
1 onion, thinly sliced
1.1 litres/2 pints pheasant stock
*   or water*
275ml/10fl oz thick or double
*   cream*

For the stuffing:
450g/1lb leeks, cooked and
*   drained*
50g/2oz butter
breadcrumbs
pecans or walnuts
marjoram
thyme
parsley

Pre-heat oven to 200°C/400°F/Gas Mark 6.

---

1 Brown pheasants in butter.

---

2 Make stuffing by tossing leeks in butter with breadcrumbs, nuts, herbs and parsley. Season well and moisten with milk if a little too dry. Spoon into pheasant and press well.

---

3 Cover pheasants with bacon and put into a roasting tin on top of vegetables. Pour on the stock or water and bake in the oven for about 1 hour.

---

4 Remove pheasants and carve, arranging meat overlapping.

---

5 Strain the pan juices and reduce to make 575ml (1 pint). Add the cream and season well. Hand the sauce separately.

Elizabeth's Pheasant and Pasta Salad

Serves 8

This is a useful recipe for summer lunches using pheasants from the freezer.

4 pheasant breasts
100g/4oz butter
250g/9oz pasta shells or bows
3 tablespoons olive oil
4 tablespoons basil, lemon thyme,
*   tarragon, chopped*
2 tablespoons lemon juice
2 cloves garlic, crushed
10 tablespoons mayonnaise
handful parsley, chopped

1 Sauté pheasant breasts in butter. Shred when cooked.

2 Meanwhile, cook the pasta in plenty of boiling water until done.

3 Make a vinaigrette with the oil, herbs, lemon juice and garlic and season well.

4 Drain pasta and pour on the vinaigrette. When cool, mix the pheasant with the mayonnaise. Scatter parsley over and serve cold.

Pheasant on Watercress Salad

Serves 6

This dish is served warm – it is a delicious way to use up frozen pheasant in the summer. You could follow this course with some very creamy pommes boulangère, or serve them at the side on flat cocotte dishes.

brace of pheasants
275ml/½ pint vinaigrette
3 eggs, hard-boiled
1 shallot, finely chopped
2 bunches watercress

1 Roast the pheasants in the usual way, with some bacon over the breast and a little extra butter for basting.

2 Make a thick vinaigrette by adding 3 yolks of hard-boiled eggs and finely chopped shallot to the basic recipe.

3 Arrange the watercress on a large platter. Carve the pheasant thinly and place on top of the watercress. Pour the vinaigrette over the pheasant and serve immediately.

Pheasant Normande

Serves 8

This is a more simple method of dealing with the classic recipe. You can use home-made apple purée from your freezer or a jar from the supermarket.

brace of pheasants
275ml/½ pint water, or pheasant
*   stock from a previous roast*
Calvados
6–8 tablespoons apple purée
150ml/¼ pint single cream
parsley

Pre-heat the oven to 200°C/400°F/Gas Mark 6.

1 Roast the pheasants in a pan with the water or stock. When cooked, remove, carve and keep warm and well covered on a meat platter.

2 Return the roasting pan to the heat and boil the liquid rapidly, stirring so that all the juices are well mixed. Add the juices from the carving.

3 Pour in a glass of Calvados and boil for 1 minute. Stir in enough apple purée to make the sauce the desired consistency and add the cream. Adjust the seasoning, add some more Calvados to taste and pour into a warm sauce-boat or jug.

4 Garnish the pheasant with parsley and decorate with feathers. Hand round the sauce separately.

Pheasant with Cointreau and Croûtons

Serves 8

This is simple and quick to make. It could be eaten as it is and followed by a salad.

brace of pheasants
550g/1¼ lb button mushrooms
450g/1lb butter
8 leeks, sliced
8 slices white bread, cubed
Cointreau
cream

1 Roast pheasant in a chicken brick with a little extra water.

2 Cook mushrooms in boiling salted water. Fry the croûtons and sauté the leeks.

3 When pheasant is cooked, remove and carve and keep warm. Mix juices, Cointreau and cream and mushrooms. Reheat and adjust the seasoning, and pour over the pheasant. Arrange the pheasant on top of the leeks and croûtons around the edge.

Pheasant with White Port, Oysters and Mushrooms

Serves 6

When they are available from good delicatessens or good supermarkets, use wild mushrooms as a variation. They also lend more flavour.

brace of pheasants
450g/1lb button mushrooms
100g/4oz butter
cream
white port
12 or more oysters
1 teaspoon cayenne pepper
seasoning

1 Cook the pheasant in a chicken brick.

2 Meanwhile, cook the mushrooms in some butter, add cream and two glasses of port and boil for 3 minutes. Add oysters and simmer until cooked. Season and add cayenne.

3 Sieve mushrooms and oysters from the sauce and keep all warm.

4 Carve pheasant (putting aside legs for a stock) and arrange on a meat dish. Run a line of mushrooms and oysters up the middle and pour sauce over. Serve immediately.

Faisan à l'Orange

Serves 4

1 pheasant
175ml/6fl oz brandy
175ml/6 fl oz white wine
2 oranges
50g/2oz sugar
175ml/6fl oz water
1 orange, divided into segments
1 bunch watercress

Pre-heat oven to 200°C/400°F/Gas Mark 6.

1 Cook the pheasant in a chicken brick with brandy and white wine in the oven
for 1 hour.

2 Cut the zest from the oranges with a julienne zester and boil in the sugar and
water until tender. Drain and reserve juice. Squeeze oranges into the juice.

3 When the pheasant is cooked, remove it and carve, and then interleave with
the orange segments. Add orange juices to the cooking juices and pour over.
Garnish with watercress.

Pheasant with Cashews

Serves 4

4 pheasant breasts on the bone
seasoned flour
100g/4oz butter
6 shallots, finely chopped
6 tomatoes, skinned, pipped and
*   sliced*
1 teaspoon cinnamon
225ml/8fl oz vermouth
stock to cover
150g/5oz cashews
75g/3oz sultanas
175–225g/6–8oz brown rice

1 Dip pheasant breasts in the seasoned flour.

2 Using a large casserole dish, brown the joints in the butter. Add the shallots, the tomatoes and the cinnamon. Cook until the shallots have softened.

3 Pour on the vermouth and stock to cover. Season. Cover and simmer until cooked (about 30 minutes). Cook rice and drain.

4 Add the cashews and sultanas and heat through well.

5 Arrange joints on a dish surrounded by the rice. Pour over the sauce.

Milton Pheasant

Serves 6

6 pheasant breasts
4 leeks, sliced
3 carrots, sliced
3 tablespoons oil
3 tomatoes, peeled and quartered
2 tablespoons tomato purée
3 cloves garlic
350ml/12fl oz red or white wine
stock
1 bay leaf
175ml/6fl oz Drambuie
175ml/6fl oz thick cream
6 croûtes of pastry

1 Shred the pheasant.

2 Using a large pan with a cover, sauté the leeks and carrots in the oil for 5 minutes. Add the pheasant and brown. Add the tomatoes, tomato purée and garlic. Season. Add wine, stock and bay leaf.

3 Flame the Drambuie in a separate pan and pour on to the pheasant. Cover the pan and simmer until the ingredients are cooked.

4 Strain the vegetables and pheasant. Reduce the liquid by one-third and add the cream. Stir in the pheasant and vegetables.

5 Serve from the pan, garnished with pastry croûtes.

Pheasant with Grand Marnier

Serves 4

1 young hen pheasant
150ml/¼ pint Grand Marnier
2 shallots, sliced
3 carrots
100g/4oz bacon, cut into lardons
stock
450g/1lb button mushrooms
2 cloves garlic
seasoning
4 tablespoons parsley

1 Cook the pheasant in the chicken brick with a little of the Grand Marnier, flamed.

2 Meanwhile, sauté the shallots, carrots and bacon until soft, cover with stock and simmer for 20 minutes. Cook mushrooms and garlic in some butter in a separate pan.

3 Remove pheasant when cooked, carve and keep warm.

4 Add any juices from carving and cooking to the vegetables and purée. Heat the remaining Grand Marnier in a separate pan and flame. Add to the sauce, adjusting the seasoning.

5 Arrange mushrooms in a band around one side of the pheasant and pour the sauce on the meat. Garnish with parsley.

Pheasant with Prawns

Serves 4

It is important that the pheasant is not too dry and that the prawns are not overcooked.

1 pheasant
175ml/6fl oz stock
1 bay leaf
18 frozen pickling onions
25g/1oz sugar
225g/½lb button mushrooms
225g/½lb prawns, cooked and
*   peeled*
150g/6oz butter
juice of 1 lemon
1 glass Madeira
salt and pepper
parsley to decorate

Pre-heat oven to 200°C/400°F/Gas Mark 6.

---

1 Brown pheasant in oil and butter in a deep casserole. Pour on stock and season, then add a bay leaf and some parsley stalks. Cover and cook in the oven for one hour.

---

2 Blanch onions for 5 minutes in boiling water. Drain, then glaze them in 50g (2oz) butter and the sugar in a pan.

---

3 Cook the mushrooms in remaining butter, lemon juice and pepper. Heat the prawns in a little pheasant juice, drain and reserve. Do not over-heat.

---

4 When the pheasant is cooked, remove and carve. Add the carving juices to the cooking liquor and reduce by one-third. Add the Madeira and taste to season. Arrange the garnish of mushrooms, onions and prawns with the carved pheasant and pour on the sauce. Decorate with chopped parsley.

Pheasant with Pears and Whisky

Serves 4

The better the blend of whisky, the more delicious this dish.

1 pheasant, jointed
4 pears
100g/4oz butter
150ml/1/4 pint white wine
100g/4oz sugar
caster sugar
stock (game or pheasant)
575ml/1 pint double cream
150ml/1/4 pint whisky

Pre-heat oven to 190°C/375°F/Gas Mark 5.

---

1 Brown fruit in hot butter, remove to pre-soaked chicken brick, add the wine and cook in the oven for 1 1/4 hours.

---

2 Make a syrup for the pears with sugar and 1/2 pint water. Poach pears, drain and dust with some caster sugar.

---

3 Boil stock to syrupy consistency, add cream, season and reheat.

---

4 Remove pheasant and arrange on a serving dish. Pour over sauce. Keep warm.

---

5 Brown the pears gently under the grill and remove to serving dish. Arrange pheasant and pears. Heat the whisky in a pan, set alight and pour over pears.

Pheasant Fricassée

Serves 4

4 pheasant breasts
75g/3oz butter
12 tiny frozen pickling onions
50g/2oz flour
275ml/½ pint Vouvray
2 cloves garlic, crushed
tarragon
1 bay leaf
225g/8oz button mushrooms
1 tablespoon brandy
125ml/4fl oz Greek yoghurt or
*   crème fraîche*

Pre-heat oven to 190°C/375°F/Gas Mark 5.

1 Sauté joints in butter in a heavy casserole until golden. Remove. Add onions, cover, and cook until tender.

2 Sprinkle on the flour and pour in the wine. Add garlic and herbs, bring to simmering and season. Add pheasant and mushrooms and cover the casserole. Bake in the oven for 45 minutes.

3 Remove pheasant and keep hot. Reduce the liquid by half, and then add the brandy and the yoghurt or crème fraîche. Pour over the pheasant.

Pheasant with Cranberry Compôte

Serves 4

An idea adapted from an American recipe for turkey.

1 pheasant
4 chicken livers
175g/6oz bacon, chopped
1 tablespoon thyme
1 tablespoon parsley
75g/3oz breadcrumbs
1 beaten egg
brandy
225g/8oz frozen cranberries
sugar
cinnamon

Pre-heat oven to 200°C/400°F/Gas Mark 6.

---

1 Mix the livers, bacon, herbs and breadcrumbs, and add the egg and the brandy to moisten. Stuff into the bird. Bake in the chicken brick for 50 minutes until cooked.

---

2 Meanwhile, simmer the fruit in water with sugar and cinnamon until soft but not falling apart.

---

3 Remove pheasant, carve and keep warm. Heat 3 tablespoons of brandy and flame; pour on to the pheasant juices and over the pheasant. Serve the compôte separately. This is best served with french fries.

Aylesbury Pheasant

Serves 4

Of course, any duck livers will do . . .

1 pheasant (and liver, chopped)
75g/3oz bacon, chopped
75g/3oz button mushrooms, finely
 chopped
1 tablespoon parsley, chopped
65g/2½oz breadcrumbs
1 beaten egg
seasoning
225g/8oz duck livers
275ml/½ pint game stock
40g/1½oz flour
25g/1oz butter
juice of 2 oranges
zest cut into strips and blanched
1 orange, cut into segments

Pr-heat oven to 200°C/400°F/Gas Mark 6.

---

1 Mix the pheasant liver with the bacon, mushrooms, parsley, breadcrumbs and bind with the egg. Season and stuff the pheasant. Bake in a chicken brick.

---

2 Meanwhile, cook the duck livers in the stock, remove and sieve. Make a sauce with the stock, flour and butter. Roughly chop the livers, and add orange juice and zest. It might be necessary to add a drop of gravy browning to improve colour.

---

3 When the pheasant is cooked, carve and keep warm. Add the juices to the sauce and heat again and pour over the pheasant.

---

4 Garnish with the orange segments. Serve hot.

Pheasant Stuffed with Oyster Mushrooms and Chives

Serves 4

Quite often I make extra stuffing and bake it in a bread tin.

pheasant (with liver, chopped)
7 rashers bacon
175g/6oz oyster mushrooms
3 tablespoons parsley, chopped
8 tablespoons chives, chopped
3 egg yolks
3 carrots, sliced
2 leeks, sliced
3 cloves garlic
stock to cover
1 glass red wine
double cream
brandy

Pre-heat oven to 200°C/400°F/Gas Mark 6.

1 Mix pheasant liver, 3 rashers bacon (chopped), and mushrooms with parsley, chives and egg yolks. Press into the pheasant.

2 Braise the vegetables in some butter and place the pheasant on top. Cover with the remaining bacon. Add water or stock and wine to cover vegetables and braise in a covered pot for one hour.

3 When the pheasant is done, remove, carve and keep warm. Interleave with stuffing.

4 Purée the vegetables, adding more stock if necessary; add some cream and brandy to taste, adjust seasoning. Hand the sauce separately.

Christmas Eve Pheasant

Serves 4

Chestnuts remind us of Christmas and this can look very festive if it is imaginatively decorated.

1 pheasant
3 petit suisse
6 Cox's apples, peeled, cored
  and grated
4 rashers bacon
450g/1lb chestnuts
50g/2oz butter
sugar
Calvados
game stock
crescents of puff pastry to
  garnish

Pre-heat oven to 200°C/400°F/Gas Mark 6.

---

1 Stuff the pheasant with 2 of the petit suisse and one grated apple, mixed together and seasoned. Cover with bacon and roast in the oven for nearly 1 hour.

---

2 Meanwhile, slit the chestnuts, place in boiling water and cook for 25 minutes. Remove their skins and reserve all but 4, which should be mashed. Cook the grated apple with some butter and a little sugar.

---

3 Mix together the mashed chestnuts, apple and the remaining petit suisse. Add the Calvados. Add enough stock to achieve the right consistency for a sauce. Season.

---

4 Remove pheasant, carve and keep warm, and decorate with puff pastry crescents and reserved chestnuts. Add the cooking juices to the sauce which may be handed separately.

Pheasant Cooked like Coq au Vin

Makes 8

A delicious way of cooking pheasant, which should be served with mashed potato and a green salad. Sometimes fried croutons can be added as a garnish.

brace of pheasants, jointed
450g/1lb bacon, cut into strips
30 tiny frozen pickling onions
50g/2oz butter
50ml/2fl oz oil
150ml/¼ pint brandy
2 tablespoons flour
¾ bottle red wine
3 tablespoons thyme
2–3 bay leaves
3 tablespoons sugar mixed with a
  little ground nutmeg
450g/1lb button mushrooms
6–8 cloves garlic, crushed

Pre-heat oven to 190°C/375°F/Gas Mark 5.

---

1 Using a heavy casserole sauté the bacon and onions in butter and oil until golden. Remove, brown the birds, pour on the brandy, heat and flame. Remove the birds. Add the flour and stir well.

---

2 Replace the pheasant, onions and bacon. Add the wine, herbs, sugar, mushrooms and garlic.

---

3 Cover the pan and cook for about one hour in the oven.

Pheasant with Grapes and Brandy

Makes 4

Another very simple recipe.

4 pheasant breasts
butter
50ml/2fl oz stock
2 tablespoons brandy
4 tablespoons fresh orange juice
450g/1lb grapes, skinned and
*   pipped*
3 tablespoons redcurrant jelly

Pre-heat oven to 200°C/400°F/Gas Mark 6.

1 Sauté breasts in the butter for 5 minutes. Add the stock, brandy and orange juice, and the grapes.

2 Cover the pan and cook in the oven for about 20 minutes.

3 Remove breasts, arrange with grapes on a serving dish and keep warm. Reduce the liquid by one-third, add the warmed redcurrant jelly and pour over. Serve immediately.

Pheasant with Olives
and Vermouth

Serves 4

Sometimes the addition of strips of anchovy helps disguise the taste of pheasant that has been hung too long.

4 pheasant breasts
4 rashers bacon, cut into strips
12 tiny frozen pickling onions
50g/2oz butter
12 stoned black olives
4 green olives
50ml/2fl oz stock
150ml/¼ pint vermouth
handful parsley, chopped

1 Sauté the bacon and onions in the butter, add the pheasant breasts, season well and cook slowly for about 15 minutes until done. Remove and arrange on a dish and keep hot.

2 Add the olives, stock and vermouth to the pan. Stir well for several minutes. Season. Pour over the pheasant and scatter chopped parsley over.

Fagiano con Limone

Serves 4

A recipe from an Italian friend who likes Chinese cooking. An unmessy way of coating in flour – put flour and meat into a bag and shake it about.

1 pheasant, cut into finger-sized
strips
4 lemons
100g/4oz plain flour
salt and pepper
4 tablespoons sunflower oil
8 tablespoons brown sugar
275ml/½ pint stock
1 tablespoon cornflour

1 Peel zest off the lemons and squeeze the juice. Marinate pheasant overnight in the lemon juice, stirring frequently.

2 Next day, pat meat dry, and then coat with seasoned flour. Fry in a heavy pan in the oil until golden.

3 Arrange in a dish and sprinkle with lemon zest and brown sugar. Mix the cornflour to a paste with a little of the stock. Heat the stock with lemon marinade and cornflour paste and hand separately in a jug.

Pheasant Breasts in Foil with Bees' Knees Sauce

Makes 4

This is basically béarnaise sauce but by leaving the shallots in it becomes bees' knees sauce. You can use dried tarragon.

4 pheasant breasts
50g/2oz butter
1 tablespoon tarragon, chopped

For the sauce:
12 peppercorns
2 shallots, chopped finely
5 tablespoons tarragon vinegar
3 tablespoons stock
5 egg yolks, beaten
225–275g/8–10oz butter
2–3 tablespoons tarragon,
    chopped

Pre-heat oven to 200°C/400°F/Gas Mark 6.

---

1 Wrap the breasts in foil with butter and tarragon and bake in the oven for 15 minutes until just done.

---

2 Meanwhile, make the sauce. Place the peppercorns tied in muslin, shallots and vinegar in a pan and reduce by half. Remove the peppercorns and add the stock and the egg yolks. Put into a bowl and beat over a pan of boiling water until thickened. Remove and beat in the butter. Finally, add the chopped tarragon and keep warm until needed. Hand the sauce separately.

Pheasant Stuffed with Sausage and Apples

Serves 4

1 pheasant
1 onion, finely chopped
175g/6oz butter
75g/3oz breadcrumbs
75g/3oz sausagemeat
2 apples, peeled and cubed
1 tablespoon each thyme and sage
8 walnuts, crushed roughly
1 glass red wine

Pre-heat oven to 200°C/400°F/Gas Mark 6.

1 Sauté the onion in the butter until transparent. Add the breadcrumbs, sausagemeat, apple, thyme and sage and walnuts. Fill into pheasant.

2 Place the pheasant in a chicken brick. Pour on the red wine and bake for one hour.

3 Remove pheasant and carve. Pour over the juices and serve at once with a green salad.

Pheasant with Wild Rice and Sultana Stuffing

Serves 4

Wild rice is a delicious and natural accompaniment to game and this stuffing helps keep the bird nice and juicy.

1 pheasant
3 rashers bacon
1 onion, finely chopped
50g/2oz walnuts, finely chopped
1 tablespoon parsley, finely
  chopped
2 tablespoons sultanas
50g/2oz cooked wild rice
2 tablespoons wholemeal
  breadcrumbs
1 egg, beaten
salt and pepper
butter for greasing tin

Pre-heat oven to 200°C/400°F/Gas Mark 6.

---

1 Make stuffing by combining onion, walnuts, parsley, sultanas, wild rice, breadcrumbs and seasoning with the beaten egg.

---

2 Spoon the stuffing into the pheasant and secure the opening with a skewer.

---

3 Cover the breast with bacon and roast in a greased tin for 50 minutes or until done.

Pheasant Pastie

Makes 4

A handy way of using up left-over pheasant – good for picnics and children's lunches.

175g/6oz cooked pheasant meat
100g/4oz potatoes, peeled and
  finely chopped
1 shallot, peeled and finely
  chopped
mixed herbs to taste
1 dessertspoon port
1 dessertspoon redcurrant jelly
225g/8oz shortcrust pastry
1 egg, beaten
salt and pepper

Pre-heat oven to 220°C/425°F/Gas Mark 7.

---

1 Combine pheasant meat, potatoes, shallot, herbs, port, redcurrant jelly and seasoning in a bowl. Set aside.

---

2 Roll out pastry to ½cm (¼in) thick on a floured board. Using a large saucer as a template, cut out 4 circles.

---

3 Place filling in the centre of each piece of pastry. Wet the edges with water, join them on the top and pinch together to form an upright frill. Prick with a fork.

---

4 Brush each pastie with beaten egg and place on a greased baking tray. Put in the hot oven for 10 minutes then reduce the heat to 180°C/350°F/Gas Mark 4 and cook for a further 30 minutes.

Eastern Surprise Pheasant

Makes 4

Time to have a bath and a drink whilst the pheasant marinades. The final cooking is so quick and easy.

4 pheasant breasts
1 clove garlic, crushed
1 tablespoon white wine vinegar
1 tablespoon water
2 teaspoons tomato purée
2 level teaspoons cornflour
2 teaspoons soy sauce
1cm (½in) piece fresh peeled
*   ginger, very finely chopped*
1 small green chilli, very finely
*   chopped*
4 spring onions, very finely
*   chopped*
150ml/¼ pint stock, made with a
*   chicken cube*
1 small red pepper, seeded and
*   cut into julienne strips*
1 small green pepper, seeded and
*   cut into julienne strips*
100g/4oz beansprouts
salt and black pepper

1 In a bowl combine garlic, vinegar, water, tomato purée, cornflour, soy sauce, ginger, chilli and onion. Season and pour over pheasant breasts. Set aside for 2 hours to allow flavours to develop.

2 Transfer to a wok or a deep frying pan, add stock, peppers and seasoning. Simmer for 10 minutes, stirring gently.

3 Add beansprouts and cook for a further 5 minutes. Serve immediately with rice.

Smoked Pheasant Salad with Raspberry Dressing

Serves 4

Smoked pheasant is delicious and unusual. If you have a friendly neighbour-hood smokehouse, see if they will prepare some for you. You can then store them in your freezer for summer picnics. Use the following recipe as a starter or as a light summer lunch.

8 generous slices of smoked
*   pheasant*
8 thin slices of Parma ham, rolled
*   into cornets*
1 avocado, thinly sliced and
*   brushed with lemon juice to*
*   prevent discolouration.*
8 leaves radicchio
4 large leaves oak leaf lettuce
4 tablespoons olive oil
1 clove garlic, crushed
1 tablespoon raspberry vinegar
25 fresh raspberries
salt and black pepper

---

1 On 4 plates make a bed with the radicchio and oak leaf lettuce. Divide the pheasant, Parma ham and avocado between the plates and arrange attractively.

---

2 Purée half the raspberries. Make the dressing by mixing together the oil, vinegar, garlic and raspberry purée. Season and stir until well blended. Pour carefully over the avocado and serve the salad immediately, garnished with the rest of the fresh raspberries.

Pheasant Stuffed with Petit Suisse

Serves 3–4

A cream cheese stuffing inside a pheasant keeps the bird marvellously succulent.

1 pheasant
3 rashers streaky bacon
3 tablespoons petit suisse
1 tablespoon parsley, finely
  chopped
1 tablespoon chives, finely
  chopped
1 tablespoon chervil, finely
  chopped
2 spring onions, finely chopped
50g/2oz button mushrooms, finely
  chopped
4 cloves garlic, unpeeled and left
  whole
150ml/¼ pint pheasant stock
150ml/¼ pint white wine
butter
salt and pepper

Pre-heat oven to 200°C/400°F/Gas Mark 6.

---

1 Combine petit suisse, herbs, onions, mushrooms and seasoning. Stuff pheasant with mixture.

---

2 Place in a greased tin, breast-down and covered by bacon. Add garlic cloves and roast for 40 minutes. Turn the right way up, remove bacon and roast for a further 10 minutes to brown.

---

3 With a spoon, scrape out all the herb mixture from the pheasant cavity and mix with the cooking juices in the tin. Squash the garlic cloves with the back of the spoon to extract juices, add to mixture, then discard skins. Carve pheasant and keep warm on a serving dish.

---

4 Add wine to the creamy cooking juices and cook over a high heat for 1 minute. Pour in stock and cook for a further 2 minutes, stirring continuously.

5 Check seasoning and serve sauce separately in a sauce-boat.

Quick Cold Pheasant

Serves 4

This really is quick!

1 cooked pheasant, all meat
   shredded
225g/8oz bought mayonnaise
1 tablespoon curry paste
¼ teaspoon ground ginger
1 tablespoon sultanas
2 eating apples, peeled, cored
   and finely chopped
2 tablespoons chopped walnuts
1 tablespoon chopped fresh
   coriander
1 tablespoon mango chutney
seasoning

1 Combine the mayonnaise with the curry paste and ground ginger, then add all
the remaining ingredients. Serve on a bed of watercress or mixed green salad.

Scrumptious Pheasant

Serves 4

1 pheasant
100g/4oz green back bacon,
  chopped
1 large onion, finely sliced
2 cloves garlic, crushed
3 tablespoons oil
50g/2oz butter
2 large cooking apples, peeled,
  cored and sliced
275ml/½ pint Somerset cider
  (Scrumpy if you can get it)
275ml/½ pint double cream
salt and pepper

Pre-heat oven to 140°C/275°F/Gas Mark 1.

---

1 Melt oil and butter in a heavy-bottomed casserole and sauté the bacon, onion and garlic. Remove and set aside.

---

2 Brown the pheasant in the casserole then surround with bacon, onion and garlic and apple slices. Pour cider over.

---

3 Cover and cook on the top of the oven until the sauce starts to bubble. Remove from heat and stir in cream and seasoning.

---

4 Cook in the oven until pheasant is done – approximately 1½ hours. Carve pheasant on to a serving dish and keep warm.

---

5 Liquidise sauce, check seasoning and pour over pheasant. Serve immediately.

Pheasant with Fresh Apricots

Serves 4

This makes a lovely and unusual dish for a dinner party.

1 pheasant
12 fresh apricots
butter
demerara sugar
1 small onion
3 tablespoons brandy
3 tablespoons Grand Marnier
450ml/16 fl oz pheasant stock
salt and black pepper

Pre-heat oven to 200°C/400°F/Gas Mark 6.

---

1 Roast pheasant, carve and keep warm. Reserve carcass and pan juices.

---

2 Meanwhile, halve all the apricots (reserving stones) and sauté 16 halves in butter. Sprinkle with sugar and brown under a hot grill. Arrange around pheasant and keep warm.

---

3 Break up carcass and put in roasting tin with juices, 1 teaspoon sugar, salt, pepper, brandy and Grand Marnier, apricot stones and remaining halves. Shake over high heat for 1 minute and add stock. Reduce liquor by half and simmer for 20 minutes.

---

4 Strain sauce and heat again until it goes syrupy. Check seasoning and pour over pheasant, leaving apricots exposed.

Pheasant with Apples and Grapes

Makes 4

1 pheasant
175g/6oz Philadelphia cream
 cheese
salt and black pepper
1 tablespoon oil
25g/1oz butter
2 large cooking apples, peeled,
 cored and diced
450g/1lb black grapes, halved
 and seeded
2 tablespoons brandy

Pre-heat oven to 200°C/400°F/Gas Mark 6.

1 Stuff the pheasant with cheese, salt and pepper. Roast in oil and butter for 50 minutes, or until done. Carve the pheasant on to serving dish and keep warm.

2 Toss the fruit in the roasting juices until just cooked and sprinkle brandy over. Adjust seasoning.

3 Arrange the fruit around the pheasant and pour over the cooking juices.

4 Cover with foil and leave to stand in a warm oven for 10 minutes before serving, to allow the flavours to develop.

Stephanie's Pheasant with Fennel Cream Sauce

Serves 3–4

The combination of pheasant and the creamy fennel sauce makes for an unusual and very subtle flavour.

1 pheasant, jointed
2–3 tablespoons flour
50g/2oz butter
275ml/½ pint pheasant stock
150ml/¼ pint white wine
1 tablespoon brandy
1 onion, finely sliced
1 large bulb fennel, finely sliced
150ml/¼ pint double cream
100g/4oz ham, cut into fine strips
1 tablespoon parsley, chopped
salt and pepper

Pre-heat oven to 180°C/350°F/Gas Mark 4.

---

1 Coat pheasant pieces in flour and sauté in butter in a heavy-bottomed casserole.

---

2 Stir in sufficient flour to absorb fat and blend in wine, brandy, stock, salt and pepper. Add fennel and onion and bring to simmering point.

---

3 Cover and put in oven for 45 minutes

---

4 Remove pheasant to a warm serving dish. Stir cream into sauce, check seasoning and pour over pheasant. Garnish with parsley and ham strips.

Pheasant Breasts in Port

Serves 2

As with all recipes that call for breast only, use the legs and carcass for a good, strong stock.

2 pheasant breasts
65g/2½oz butter
2 rashers back bacon, cut into
    strips
50g/2oz button mushrooms, finely
    sliced
225ml/8fl oz port
225ml/8fl oz pheasant stock
4 small triangles of fried bread
salt and pepper

1 Gently fry pheasant breasts in 25g (1oz) butter for 10 minutes, turning regularly. Remove to serving dish and keep warm.

2 Sauté bacon and mushrooms in the same fat. Remove with a slotted spoon and scatter over the pheasant breasts. Deglaze pan with port and over a high heat reduce by half. Add stock and reduce liquid again until it becomes syrupy. Mix in remaining butter, a little at a time, stirring vigorously, until the sauce looks rich and shiny.

3 Check seasoning and pour over pheasant. Garnish with fried bread triangles.

Pheasant Pudding

Serves 4–6

A good, old-fashioned, hearty meal – ideal for a shoot lunch.

225g/8oz suet crust (standard
  recipe)
1 old cock pheasant, all meat
  stripped from bone and cut
  into bite-sized pieces
100g/4oz rump steak cut into 1cm
  (½in) squares
plain flour
50g/2oz mushrooms, sliced
½ onion, chopped
1 tablespoon parsley, chopped
1 teaspoon sage, chopped
1 glass port
275ml/½ pint pheasant stock
butter
salt and pepper

1 Butter a 2-pint pudding basin. Roll out suet crust pastry to ½cm (¼in) thickness and line basin. Roll out remainder to make a lid and set aside.

2 Toss the pheasant meat and steak in sufficient flour to coat and season well.

3 Fill the basin with meat, mushrooms, onion, herbs and port. Add enough stock to cover the meat. Cover with the suet lid and seal by pinching the edges.

4 Cover the pudding with buttered greaseproof paper secured with string, and again with a pudding cloth tied tightly with the knot on top.

5 Place in a large saucepan of sufficient boiling water to reach two-thirds of the way up the basin but not to boil over its top. Keep a kettle of boiling water to top up the saucepan when necessary. Boil for 3 hours.

6 Turn out on to a warm serving dish (slide a palette knife between the crust and the basin if the pudding is unwilling to emerge). Serve with seasonal British vegetables and a pint of your local beer.

Boned Pheasant with Hazelnut Stuffing

Serves 6

A kind butcher will bone your pheasant for you if you give him some warning. This recipe then becomes quite simple and is well worth the effort.

1 pheasant, boned
3 slices streaky bacon
1 onion, thinly sliced
1 clove garlic, crushed
225ml/8fl oz pheasant stock
2 tablespoons double cream
2 tablespoons Greek yoghurt
50g/2oz butter
salt and pepper

For the stuffing:
225g/8oz minced veal
175g/6oz chicken livers, finely
*   chopped*
50g/2oz roasted hazelnuts, finely
*   chopped*
2 tablespoons parsley
1 tablespoon brandy

1 Make stuffing by combining veal, livers, hazelnuts, parsley, brandy and seasoning.

2 Lay pheasant out flat, season and put stuffing in centre. Sew up bird into a neat 'pheasant-like' shape with a trussing needle and thread. Place bacon on 'breast' and secure with string.

3 Melt the butter in a casserole and brown pheasant all over. Add onion, garlic and stock, bring to the boil, then reduce heat to low. Cover and simmer for approximately 1 hour or until done.

4 Remove the pheasant to a warmed serving dish and discard bacon and string.

5 Reduce the cooking liquid by one-third. Remove from the heat and carefully stir in the combined cream and Greek yoghurt. Check seasoning and serve separately in a sauce-boat with the pheasant.

Pheasant and Juniper Berry Casserole

Serves 4

Juniper berries are a natural flavouring for game – here they are added to a lovely, rich, warming casserole which is best served simply with mashed potatoes and buttered carrots.

1 pheasant, jointed
125ml/4fl oz oil
100g/4oz streaky bacon, rind
*   removed and chopped*
1 carrot, chopped
1 onion, chopped
2–3 tablespoons flour
425ml/¾ pint pheasant stock
4 tomatoes, skinned, seeded and
*   chopped (or one small can*
*   tomatoes)*
2 tablespoons tomato purée
1 glass port
1 teaspoon mixed chopped herbs
1 clove of garlic, crushed
10 juniper berries, crushed
salt and black pepper

Pre-heat oven to 170°C/325°F/Gas Mark 3.

---

1 In a casserole brown the pheasant, bacon, carrot and onion with the oil. Stir in enough flour to absorb fat, then blend in stock.

---

2 Add all the remaining ingredients and bring to the boil for 2 minutes. Check seasoning, cover and cook in the oven for 50 minutes.

Pheasant in Madeira Sauce

Serves 4

1 pheasant, jointed
15g/½oz flour
½ teaspoon chopped sage
75g/3oz butter
175g/6oz small button mushrooms
200ml/7fl oz Madeira
½ teaspoon freshly chopped
*   herbs*
salt and black pepper

Pre-heat oven to 190°C/375°F/Gas Mark 5.

1 Sprinkle pheasant joints with flour and sage and sauté, then brown, in 40g (1½oz) butter.

2 In a casserole, melt remaining butter and soften mushrooms; add pheasant joints, wine, herbs and seasoning. Cover, bring to simmering point then cook in the oven for 1 hour.

Pheasant on a Cabbage Bed

Serves 4

The combination of cabbage and pheasant makes a delicious and traditional meal.

1 pheasant, jointed
6 slices streaky bacon, rind
    removed, cut into lardons
50g/2oz butter
150ml/¼ pint white wine
150ml/¼ pint pheasant stock
1 teaspoon caraway seeds
half a savoy cabbage, shredded
salt and pepper

1 In a casserole, sauté pheasant and bacon with butter until cooked. Remove pheasant and keep warm.

2 Put wine, stock and caraway seeds into casserole and scrape up all the meat juices. Check seasoning and reduce liquid by one-third.

3 Add cabbage and cook until just done and still slightly crisp.

4 Remove cabbage and bacon with a slotted spoon to a warm serving dish and put pheasant on to 'bed'. Pour over cooking liquid and serve immediately.

Pheasant Breasts with Fresh Figs

Serves 2

Baking the pheasant in foil parcels really helps to keep in the moisture – it achieves results not unlike a chicken brick.

2 pheasant breasts
50g/2oz butter
6 fresh figs
150ml/¼ pint red wine
1 tablespoon caster sugar
150ml/¼ pint pheasant stock
50g/2oz mushrooms, finely
  minced
1 tablespoon crème fraîche
salt and pepper

Pre-heat oven to highest setting.

---

1 Brush pheasant breasts with 25g (1oz) melted butter, season and wrap in foil parcels. Roast for approximately 15 minutes or until just done. Keep warm.

---

2 Meanwhile, in a saucepan, dissolve the sugar in red wine over a low heat and then gently poach the figs for 2 minutes. Remove figs and reduce liquid by one-quarter.

---

3 Soften mushrooms in 25g (1oz) butter, add stock and wine, season, then gently stir in crème fraîche (add a little mushroom and wine mixture to crème fraîche first to prevent curdling).

---

4 Arrange pheasant breasts and figs cut open to look like flowers, then pour sauce over pheasant.

Savoury Pheasant Pie

Serves 4

Never feel guilty about buying ready-made pastry!

1 pheasant, meat stripped from
*   carcass*
50g/2oz belly pork, chopped
225g/½lb mushrooms
flour
salt and pepper
450g/1lb ready-made puff pastry

For the marinade:
1 onion, chopped
1 stick celery, chopped
2 sprigs parsley, chopped
7 coriander seeds
7 juniper berries
2 bay leaves
pinch marjoram
275ml/½ pint red wine
75ml/3fl oz olive oil

Pre-heat oven to 190°C/375°F/Gas Mark 5.

1 Mix together all the ingredients for the marinade, pour over pheasant meat and leave overnight.

2 The pie filling is best pre-cooked. The next day, fry the pork and mushrooms in the butter and stir in sufficient flour to absorb the fat.

3 Remove the pheasant from the marinade, strain the liquid and blend with the pork and mushrooms.

4 Add the pheasant and seasoning. Cover and simmer for 1 hour. When cooked, put into a deep pie dish and allow to cool slightly.

5 Meanwhile, roll out pastry to ½cm (¼in) thickness. Cut off 1cm (½in) wide strips and place them round the dampened rim of the dish, brush with water and cover pie with remaining pastry. Trim, press down edges to seal and decorate as you fancy – mini pheasants made from left-over bits of pastry if you are artistic – brush with beaten egg and bake for about 30 minutes until golden-brown.

Paprika Pheasant

Serves 4

This is a favourite paprika chicken recipe which works very well for pheasant.

1 pheasant
450g/1lb onions, finely chopped
2 tablespoons tomato purée
4 tablespoons paprika
2 teaspoons caster sugar
3 dessertspoons flour
50g/2oz butter
275ml/½ pint red wine
275ml/½ pint pheasant stock
275ml/½ pint sour cream
2 tablespoons chopped parsley

Pre-heat oven to 180°C/350°F/Gas Mark 4.

1 Brown pheasant and onions in a casserole with the butter.

2 In a small bowl blend tomato purée, paprika, sugar and flour. Stir in 2 tablespoons hot stock.

3 Add tomato purée mixture, remaining stock and wine to casserole. Season. Cover and bake for 50 minutes.

4 Remove pheasant, cover and keep warm.

5 Stir a little of the sauce into the sour cream to prevent curdling then add cream to casserole. Allow to blend thoroughly then pour over pheasant.

6 Serve garnished with chopped parsley.

Louise's Georgian Pheasant

Serves 4

This is our slightly simpler version of one of the greatest ways of serving pheasant. It goes perfectly with the nutty flavour of wild rice.

1 pheasant
225g/8oz walnut halves
900g/2lb seedless white grapes
juice of 4 blood oranges
150ml/¼ pint China tea
150ml/¼ pint sweet white wine
40g/1½oz butter
275ml/½ pint crème fraiche
salt and black pepper

Pre-heat oven to 190°C/375°F/Gas Mark 5.

---

1 Pour boiling water over the walnuts and put them into a low (Gas Mark 1–2) oven for 10 minutes. This soaks away all the dark bitter juices from the skins. Strain and rinse the now pale walnuts and set aside.

---

2 Meanwhile, liquidise the grapes and sieve the juice.

---

3 Put pheasant into a casserole with the walnut halves, grape juice, orange juice, tea, wine, butter and seasoning. Cook in the oven for 50 minutes.

---

4 Remove the pheasant, carve on to a serving dish and keep warm.

---

5 Reduce the cooking juices by half then liquidise. Put a little of the mixture with the crème fraiche then add all the cream to the sauce. Stir gently until thoroughly blended. Check seasoning.

---

6 Pour some sauce over pheasant, handing extra around in a sauce-boat. Serve immediately with wild rice.

Pheasant with Seville Sauce

Serves 4

This is a marvellous sauce and well worth all the preparation.

1 pheasant
2 Seville oranges, peeled and
*   quartered*
50g/2oz butter

For the sauce:
1 large onion, finely sliced
1 stick celery, finely sliced
50g/2oz mushrooms, finely
*   chopped*
2 rashers streaky bacon, finely
*   chopped*
100g/4oz carrots, finely chopped
50g/2oz dripping
3–4 dessertspoons flour
150ml/¼ pint red wine
150ml/¼ pint tomato juice
150–275ml/¼–½ pint pheasant
*   stock*
juice and grated peel of 2 Seville
*   oranges*
juice and grated peel of 1 lemon
½ teaspoon mixed herbs
2 dessertspoons redcurrant jelly
1 glass port
salt and black pepper

---

1 Stuff the pheasant with the peeled and quartered oranges and roast with the butter until done – about 50 minutes.

---

2 To make the sauce sauté all the vegetables in the dripping until just golden. Stir in enough flour to absorb the fat then blend in the wine, tomato juice and 150ml (¼ pint) of stock. Bring to the boil slowly, stirring all the time. Add herbs, seasoning, orange and lemon juices and grated rinds. Cover pan and simmer until vegetables are done.

---

3 When the pheasant is ready, remove to a serving dish, carve and keep warm.

4 Scrape the cooking juices from the roasting tin with a little stock and add to the Seville sauce. Add redcurrant jelly and port.

5 Pour over pheasant and serve extra sauce in a sauce-boat.

Creamy Pheasant

Serves 4

1 pheasant, jointed
50g/2oz butter
150ml/¼ pint stock, made from a
   chicken stock cube
2 tablespoons redcurrant jelly
275ml/½ pint double cream
1 tablespoon brandy
chopped parsley
salt and black pepper

Pre-heat oven to 170°C/325°F/Gas Mark 3.

---

1 In a casserole fry the pheasant joints in butter until brown. Add stock, cover and cook in the oven until done – about 45 minutes.

---

2 Remove the pheasant and keep warm. Quickly reduce the stock by half.

---

3 Stir in the redcurrant jelly then the cream. Flame the brandy then add to the sauce.

---

4 Check seasoning, pour sauce over pheasant and serve garnished with plenty of chopped parsley.

Tandoori Pheasant

Serves 4

As this recipe can be prepared well in advance, it is a useful one to remember when rushed evenings loom!

1 pheasant, skinned and jointed
3 cloves garlic, crushed
1¼ teaspoons chilli powder
½ teaspoon ginger
½ teaspoon turmeric
½ teaspoon salt
25ml/1fl oz lemon juice
200ml/7fl oz plain yoghurt
2 teaspoons coriander powder
1 teaspoon cumin powder
1 teaspoon paprika
50g/2oz butter, melted
salt

Pre-heat oven to 200°C/400°F/Gas Mark 6.

---

1 Mix together garlic, 1 teaspoon chilli powder, ginger, turmeric, a pinch of salt and sufficient water to make a paste.

---

2 Dry the pheasant carefully with a kitchen towel, then with a sharp knife make 2 or 3 diagonal slits in each piece.

---

3 Rub the chilli paste thoroughly into the pheasant joints then set them aside to marinate for 1 hour.

---

4 Meanwhile, mix together the yoghurt, the remaining spices, the lemon juice and any left-over chilli paste. Pour over the pheasant and leave in the refrigerator overnight to allow the flavours to penetrate the meat.

---

5 The next day, remove the pheasant from the marinade and place on a baking tray brushed with some of the melted butter. Pour the remaining butter over the meat and roast in the oven for approximately 20 minutes or until done. Serve immediately with brown rice and a mixed salad.

Sweet Pheasant Curry

Serves 4

1 pheasant, jointed
2 onions, chopped
2 cloves garlic, crushed
1 eating apple, peeled and sliced
2 carrots, grated
425g/15oz can of mangoes
2 tablespoons curry paste
1 tablespoon plain flour
50g/2oz butter
275ml/½ pint pheasant stock
1 tablespoon desiccated coconut
2 tablespoons sultanas
2 tablespoons mango chutney
salt

1 Sauté the onions and garlic in the butter until just soft then add the apple, carrots, mangoes, curry paste and flour. Continue cooking for 10 minutes then stir in the stock and mango juice from the can. Cook for a further couple of minutes. Finally, add the coconut, sultanas, chutney and pheasant pieces. Stir well, season and cover. Simmer gently for about 1 hour or until the pheasant is done.

2 Serve with saffron rice, a salad of chopped spring onions and chopped tomatoes, poppadoms and lots of chutney.

Pheasant Madras

Serves 4

A deliciously spicy curry that is very easy to prepare.

450g/1lb pheasant meat, cut into
  1cm (¹/₂in) pieces
150ml/¹/₄ pint plain yoghurt
2 onions, thinly sliced
2 large tomatoes, skinned and
  chopped
2 dried red chillies, finely
  chopped
¹/₂ teaspoon ginger
3 cloves garlic, crushed
2 teaspoons coriander powder
2 teaspoons turmeric powder
2 teaspoons cumin powder
25g/1oz butter
2 tablespoons tomato purée
150ml/¹/₄ pint coconut milk
2 large boiled potatoes, peeled
  and diced
50g/2oz frozen peas
salt

1 Mix together the pheasant and yoghurt and set aside for 1 hour.

2 Sauté the onion, chillies and garlic for 3 minutes then add the pheasant and yoghurt and cook for a further 10 minutes. Stir in the ginger, coriander, turmeric, cumin, tomatoes, tomato purée and coconut milk and simmer for 5 minutes, stirring continuously.

3 Add the potatoes and peas and cook gently until they are heated through. Add salt to taste, transfer to a warm dish and serve with rice and a tomato, onion and cucumber salad.

Pheasant with Smoked Bacon and Sloe Gin

Serves 4

It is rather nice if your pheasant and sloe gin are both home-grown and you serve the dish with your own vegetables.

1 pheasant, jointed into 8 small
  pieces
8 rashers smoked streaky bacon
black pepper
5 tablespoons double cream
2 tablespoons sloe gin

For the marinade:
850ml/1½ pints red wine
2 carrots, diced
½ onion, diced
1 clove
1 clove of garlic, unpeeled but
  crushed
1 bouquet garni
25g/1oz butter
1 tablespoon flour
850ml/1½ pints pheasant stock

1 Sprinkle pheasant with black pepper, then wrap each piece with a slice of bacon. Secure with cocktail sticks. Put them in a bowl with all the marinade ingredients and leave overnight.

2 The following day, drain the pheasant, pat dry with kitchen towel and fry in a casserole in butter until brown all over. Mix in strained vegetables from marinade and flour, stir well and cook for 5 minutes. Add marinade wine and stock and simmer uncovered for 30 minutes.

3 Strain the pheasant and put in a warmed serving dish. Remove cocktail sticks.

4 Add sloe gin to liquid and reduce by half. Gently stir in cream, then strain sauce over pheasant.

Pheasant Pancakes

Serves 4

A quick and easy 'left-over' dish – ideal for a light supper in front of the television. Make your own pancakes in large batches and freeze them with greaseproof paper between the layers – they are bound to come in handy.

225g/8oz cooked pheasant meat,
  finely chopped
1 small onion, finely chopped
50g/2oz butter
2 teaspoons curry powder
1 tablespoon sultanas
1 eating apple, peeled, cored and
  chopped
1 tablespoon pine kernels
275ml/½ pint stock made from a
  chicken stock cube
1 tablespoon flour
150ml/¼ pint double cream
4 large ready-made French
  crêpes or 8 home-made
  pancakes
salt and pepper

1 In a frying pan, sauté the onion with 25g (1oz) butter until soft then add 1 teaspoon curry powder. Cook for 1 minute. Add the sultanas, apple, pine kernels, pheasant and a little stock to moisten. Cook for a few minutes or until the apple becomes soft. Season.

2 Stuff the crêpes or pancakes with this mixture and keep warm in a serving dish.

3 In the same frying pan make the sauce by melting the remaining butter and stirring in the flour and the rest of the curry powder. Cook for 1 minute. Blend in the stock and cook until you have a smooth sauce – about 8 minutes. Stir in the cream, check the seasoning and cook gently until thoroughly heated through. Pour the sauce over the crêpes or pancakes and serve immediately.

Pheasant Breasts with Mustard Cream

Serves 2

An unusual-sounding combination that works rather well!

2 pheasant breasts
75g/3oz butter
4 teaspoons french mustard
1 tablespoon white wine vinegar
1 dessertspoon tarragon vinegar
2 tablespoons double cream
cayenne pepper
salt and pepper

Pre-heat oven to 200°C/400°F/Gas Mark 6.

1 Dot the pheasant breast with 25g (1oz) butter, season and wrap in foil. Bake in the oven for about 15 minutes – or until done.

2 Meanwhile, make the sauce by melting the remaining butter in a bain-marie. Stir in the mustard, then the wine vinegar and tarragon vinegar. Cook for 8 minutes then add the cream and seasoning.

3 Place the pheasant breasts in a serving dish and pour over the sauce. Sprinkle with cayenne pepper and serve immediately.

Left-Over Pie

Serves 4

Definitely popular with the children and a good way of getting them to finish up the remains of last night's roast pheasant.

450g/1lb minced cooked pheasant
meat
1 large onion, finely chopped
2 cloves garlic, crushed
50g/2oz butter
4 tomatoes, peeled and chopped
(or one small can tomatoes)
1 tablespoon parsley, finely
chopped
1 glass red wine (optional)
450g/1lb mashed potato
salt and pepper

Pre-heat oven to 200°C/400°F/Gas Mark 6.

1 Sauté the onion and garlic in the butter until soft. Add the tomatoes, parsley and wine, and cook for 2 minutes. Finally, add the pheasant and seasoning. Cook for 2 minutes.

2 Put the meat mixture into a pie dish and cover with mashed potato. Cook in the oven for 30 minutes.

Roast Pheasant with Plum Stuffing

Serves 4

1 pheasant
3 rashers streaky bacon
150ml/¼ pint red wine
150ml/¼ pint pheasant stock

For the stuffing:
1 onion, finely chopped
50g/2oz hazelnuts, finely chopped
1 stick celery, finely sliced
50g/2oz butter
6 plums, stoned and chopped
juice from 1 orange
1 tablespoon grated orange rind
2 tablespoons brown
  breadcrumbs
salt and pepper

Pre-heat oven to 220°C/425°F/Gas Mark 7.

---

1 Make the stuffing by softening onion and celery in butter. Remove to a bowl and combine with all other ingredients. Season.

---

2 Stuff pheasant with mixture and truss. Cover with bacon rashers, season and roast for 50 minutes or until cooked.

---

3 Remove to serving dish and keep warm. Make gravy by deglazing pan with wine and stock, reduce and serve separately in a sauce-boat.

Pheasant and Prune Casserole

Serves 4

This is an adaptation of an old pork and prune recipe – it is light and creamy and really rather good.

1 pheasant, all meat stripped
  from bone
1 onion, chopped
50g/2oz butter
1 tablespoon flour
575ml/1 pint cider
225g/8oz prunes, stoned
2 cooking apples, peeled, cored
  and sliced
3 potatoes, peeled and thinly
  sliced
3 tablespoons chopped fresh sage
200ml/7fl oz double cream
salt and black pepper

Pre-heat oven to 170°C/325°F/Gas Mark 3.

1 Toss pheasant meat in seasoned flour and brown with onion in butter. Stir in cider and cook for 5 minutes.

2 Transfer to a heavy-bottomed casserole, and add all the remaining ingredients except for the cream. Cook in the oven for 50 minutes.

3 Stir in the cream. Check seasoning and return to the oven for a further 10 minutes.

Faisan à la Gourmande

Serves 4

Rather an extravagant and rich dish for a special occasion.

1 pheasant
4 round pieces of bread cut with a
  5cm (2in) diameter pastry
  cutter
50g/2oz butter
50g/2oz pâté de foie gras
1 tablespoon double cream
3 tablespoons brandy
4 tablespoons port
275ml/½ pint red wine
1 teaspoon lemon juice
salt and pepper

1 Roast pheasant, carve on to serving dish and keep warm.

2 Meanwhile, fry rounds of bread in butter. Drain on kitchen towel and set aside.

3 Blend pâté, cream, 1 teaspoon of brandy and seasoning into a smooth paste and spread half on to croûtons. Keep warm.

4 Put the wine, port and remaining brandy into the roasting tin and scrape up the cooking juices. Reduce by half. Add lemon juice, sieve and whisk in remaining pâté mixture until you have a rich smooth sauce. Check seasoning.

5 Pour sauce over pheasant and serve with garnished croûtons.

114

Pheasant Mistral

Serves 4

1 pheasant, jointed
1 onion, chopped
1 tablespoon olive oil
2 cloves garlic, crushed
1 teaspoon parsley, chopped
juice of 1 orange
125ml/4fl oz white wine
2 tablespoons tomato purée
100g/4oz black olives, stoned and
    chopped
salt and black pepper

1 Sauté pheasant joints and onion in oil until golden.

2 Add all remaining ingredients, cover and simmer for 1 hour, stirring occasionally. Check seasoning and serve immediately.

Pheasant in Creamy Garlic Sauce

Serves 2

2 pheasant breasts
15g/¹/₂oz butter
2 rashers back bacon, rind
*   removed and chopped*
1 shallot, finely chopped
125ml/¹/₄ pint double cream
2 cloves garlic, crushed
2 tablespoons chopped parsley
salt and pepper

1 Melt butter and sauté shallot and bacon in a small frying pan. Add cream, garlic, salt and pepper. Cook gently for 3 minutes.

2 Stir in pheasant breasts and parsley, making sure pheasant is covered by sauce. Cover and simmer for 10 minutes. Check seasoning and serve immediately.

Pheasant Salad with Sauce Maltaise

Serves 4

Often the mayonnaise is flavoured with juice from a blood orange.

1 pheasant
juice of 1 orange
275ml/¹/₂ pint mayonnaise
1 bunch watercress, roughly
  chopped
75g/3oz split almonds
75g/3oz currants, soaked in
  warm tea for several hours
25g/1oz celeriac, grated
seasoning

Pre-heat oven to 200°C/400°F/Gas Mark 6.

---

1 Bake the pheasant in the chicken brick (*see* page 42). Remove and allow to cool.

---

2 Shred the meat in strips.

---

3 Mix orange juice and mayonnaise in a bowl and stir in all the ingredients. Season. Arrange in a salad bowl and refrigerate until serving.

Pheasant with Baby Turnips

Serves 4

1 pheasant
75g/3oz butter
275ml/½ pint white wine
275ml/½ pint pheasant stock
1 tablespoon mixed herbs,
*   chopped*
15 small pickling onions, trimmed
*   but left whole*
675g/1½lb baby turnips, trimmed
*   and left whole*
½ teaspoon lemon juice
1 tablespoon flour
1 tablespoon parsley, chopped
50ml/2fl oz double cream
salt and pepper

Pre-heat oven to 220°C/425°F/Gas Mark 7.

---

1 Melt 40g (1½oz) butter in a large casserole and brown the pheasant all over. Pour in wine, stock, mixed herbs, and seasoning, bring to the boil, cover and cook in the oven for 30 minutes.

---

2 Meanwhile, melt remaining butter in a frying pan and sauté onions and turnips until just golden. Sprinkle flour over and stir well.

---

3 Arrange the vegetables around the pheasant in the casserole, add the lemon juice and stir gently to blend the flour and liquid. Turn down the oven temperature to 170°C/325°F/Gas Mark 3, return the casserole for 45 minutes – 1 hour or until the pheasant is done.

---

4 Transfer the pheasant and vegetables to a serving dish and keep warm.

---

5 Reduce the liquid rapidly by one-third. Remove from the heat and stir in the cream. Check seasoning and strain the sauce over the pheasant. Serve decorated with chopped parsley.

Pheasant with Lemon and Ginger

Makes 4

The lemon and soy sauce season the meat and the sauce, and the ginger gives an unusual and interesting flavour.

4 pheasant breasts
4 tablespoons soy sauce
2 tablespoons sherry
2 lemons
425ml/¾ pint stock
4 teaspoons cornflour
3 teaspoons honey
sunflower oil
2–3 cloves garlic, crushed
1 root ginger, peeled and grated

1 Marinate the breasts in soy sauce and sherry for 1 hour.

2 Using a zester pare the lemon rind and reserve. Squeeze the juice into a bowl and mix in the stock and cornflour, then stir in the honey and the juices from the marinade.

3 Using a heavy pan gently brown the breasts in some oil. Remove.

4 Sauté the garlic and ginger for 1 minute. Return the meat to the pan and add the lemon rind. Pour on the sauce and simmer for about 15 minutes or until done. Serve with rice.

Devilled Picnic Pheasant

Serves 4

This is an extremely easy recipe and is marvellous stuffed inside pitta bread.

1 pheasant
1 tablespoon boiling watee
2 tablespoons fresh coriander,
    finely chopped
1 tablespoon fresh chervil, finely
    chopped
1 tablespoon fresh chives, finely
    chopped
1 small onion
175ml/6fl oz olive oil
50ml/2fl oz white wine vinegar
2 tablespoons tomato ketchup
1 tablespoon Worcestershire
    sauce
1 teaspoon cayenne pepper
salt and black pepper

Pre-heat oven to 200°C/400°F/Gas Mark 6.

---

1 Roast pheasant, strip all the meat from the bone, set aside in a bowl and allow to cool.

---

2 Put boiling water into roasting tin and scrape up cooking juices – pour off any fat.

---

3 Put liquid in food processor with all remaining ingredients and mix until thoroughly blended.

---

4 Check seasoning and combine with pheasant meat. Allow to stand for a couple of hours at room temperature to allow flavours to develop. Serve cool with bread and a crisp green salad.

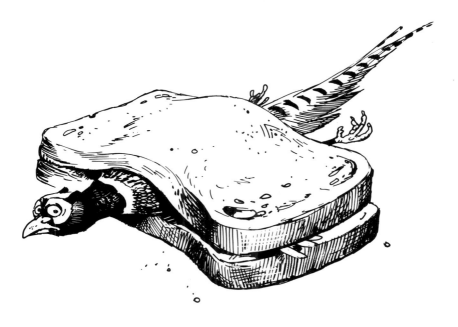

Pheasant Satay Starter

Serves 8

Serve as a first course or as an unusual cocktail party dip.

450g/1lb pheasant meat cut into
*   2.5×1cm (1in×¼in) strips*
1 onion, quartered
2 cloves garlic
4 stalks lemon grass, finely
*   chopped*
¼ teaspoon fresh ginger
1 teaspoon coriander powder
1 teaspoon cumin powder
2 teaspoons sugar
50ml/2fl oz cold water
oil for basting
salt and pepper

For the satay sauce:
1 onion, chopped
2 cloves garlic, chopped
8 dried red chillies, chopped
150g/5oz dark roast peanuts,
*   chopped*
25ml/1fl oz coconut milk
1 tablespoon soy sauce
50ml/2fl oz oil
50ml/2fl oz lemon juice
25g/1oz brown sugar
150ml/¼ pint cold water
salt and pepper

---

1 Prepare the meat by cutting into strips. Blend together in a food processor the onion, garlic, lemon grass, ginger, coriander, cumin, sugar, water and seasoning.

---

2 In a bowl, mix this paste into the pheasant making sure each piece is well coated, then set aside to marinate for 2 hours.

---

3 Prepare the sauce. Put the onion, garlic, chillies, peanuts, coconut milk, soy sauce and seasoning into a food processor and blend well.

4 Fry this paste in the oil for 5 minutes, then stir in the lemon juice, sugar and water. Simmer until the sauce thickens.

5 Meanwhile, cook the pheasant meat by putting the pieces on to small wooden skewers or cocktail sticks, brush with oil and grill for about 8 minutes, turning frequently, until done.

6 Arrange the skewers on a plate around a bowl of hot Satay Sauce as a dip, or on individual plates with a spoonful of sauce and garnished with cucumber and slices of raw onion.

Mrs Harrisson's Pheasant

Serves 4

This recipe was recommended to us as a very good way of cooking rather badly damaged birds. It comes from *The Evening Standard Book of Menus* (published by Heinemann in 1935), which we quote here; Mrs Harrisson says, however, that she always finds the cooking takes longer than thrity to thirty-five minutes – usually nearer to one hour.

1 pheasant
butter
1 tablespoon brandy
1 glass fumet of game (stock)
2 glasses cream
salt and pepper

'Flour a pheasant trussed for roasting, season it inside with salt and pepper and brown it on all sides in butter. Put the saucepan in a moderate oven and go on cooking the bird, basting often for thirty to thirty-five minutes, according to size.

When the pheasant is cooked, remove it, put in the pan a tablespoonful of brandy, a glass of fumet of game, and two glasses of cream. Cook for two or three minutes and reduce. Put back the bird, stir and baste well. Cook for a few minutes more and serve in the same saucepan or casserole in which it has been cooked.'

Index